A Clinician's Brief Guide to the Coroner's Court and Inquests

Clinician's Brief Guides

The Clinician's Brief Guides series from the Royal College of Psychiatrists and Cambridge University Press takes complex medico-legal topics and breaks them down into accessible handbooks for the busy clinician.

Other volumes in this series include:

A Clinician's Brief Guide to Dementia and the Law (2023): Brindle, Kennedy, Walsh, Alderson
ISBN: 9781911623243

A Clinician's Brief Guide to the Mental Health Act 5th edition (2022): Zigmond, Brindle
ISBN: 9781009178303

A Clinician's Brief Guide to Children's Mental Health Law (2016): Huline-Dickens
ISBN: 9781909726710

A Clinician's Brief Guide to the Mental Capacity Act 2nd edition (2015): Brindle, Branton, Stansfield, Zigmond
ISBN: 9781909726420

A Clinician's Brief Guide to the Coroner's Court and Inquests

Edited by

Gabrielle Pendlebury
Child and Adolescent Psychiatrist

Derek Tracy
South London and Maudsley NHS Foundation Trust

CAMBRIDGE
UNIVERSITY PRESS

Shaftesbury Road, Cambridge CB2 8EA, United Kingdom

One Liberty Plaza, 20th Floor, New York, NY 10006, USA

477 Williamstown Road, Port Melbourne, VIC 3207, Australia

314–321, 3rd Floor, Plot 3, Splendor Forum, Jasola District Centre, New Delhi – 110025, India

103 Penang Road, #05-06/07, Visioncrest Commercial, Singapore 238467

Cambridge University Press is part of Cambridge University Press & Assessment, a department of the University of Cambridge.

We share the University's mission to contribute to society through the pursuit of education, learning and research at the highest international levels of excellence.

www.cambridge.org
Information on this title: www.cambridge.org/9781009450096

DOI: 10.1017/9781009450102

First published 2025

A catalogue record for this publication is available from the British Library.

A Cataloging-in-Publication data record for this book is available from the Library of Congress.

ISBN 978-1-009-45009-6 Paperback

'Healthcare professionals called to give evidence in coroners' inquests may find the anticipation and the reality daunting. This guide demystifies and explains the process and offers reassurance and practical advice to minimise clinicians' concerns and ensure that their understanding of their duties and responsibilities to the court are clear and unambiguous.'

Professor Jason Payne-James, Specialist in Forensic & Legal Medicine and Consultant Forensic Physician; Lead Medical Examiner, Norfolk & Norwich University Hospital

'I read *A Clinician's Brief Guide to the Coroner's Court and Inquests* with interest. I have attended the coroner's court several times over my medical career, with varying amounts of support and guidance. I do wish my 28-year-old self had had access to such a useful real-world guide, written with such practicality and humanity. The court is complex, serving the law, the bereaved families, and future patients in terms of lessons learned. The guide takes you through this with expert contributors in a way that is both readable and clear, and would make the experience better for all potential professional attendees, and help them to serve the multilayered mission of the court to families, the law and future users of our health services. It will be a useful reference for health professionals for years to come and fills an important gap in the literature.'

Dr Chris Streather, Regional Medical Director NHSE London

Figure 0.1 Coroner's court.
Courtesy of Tony Rollinson.

Thank you to Mark, Sunita and Arun for their patience and to the London Library for its serenity.

Figure 0.2 Inquest.
Courtesy of Tony Rollinson.

Contents

Contributors

Stephanie Bridger
Chief Nurse, West London NHS Trust

Lydia Brown
Acting Senior Coroner for West London

Dr Elaine Chung
Child and Adolescent Psychiatrist, South London and Maudsley NHS Foundation Trust

Sonya Clinch
Clinical Director, West London NHS Trust

Eva Ferlez
Head of Patient Safety & Effective Practice, West London NHS Trust

Emma Galland
Partner & Solicitor-Advocate, Healthcare and Public Law, Hill Dickinson LLP

Karen Hall
Specialist Nurse in Tissue Donation

Dr Christopher Hilton
Chief Operating Officer, West London NHS Trust

Gillian Kelly
Interim Chief Nurse, West London NHS Trust

Dr Sian McIver
Adult Psychiatrist and Magistrate

Arif Naqvi
Archivist, Gothenburg, Sweden

Dr Shaun O'Connell
General Practitioner and Commissioner

Professor Keith Rix
Visiting Professor of Medical Jurisprudence, University of Chester

Tony Rollinson
Graphic Artist

Professor Carol Seymour
Emeritus Professor of Clinical Biochemistry and Metabolic Medicine, St George's Hospital Medical School

Dr Sunita Shridhar
General Practitioner

Dr Mark Tarn
Consultant Occupational Health Psychiatrist, Parliamentary Health & Wellbeing Service

Shirley Tench
Mental Health Social Worker, Nottinghamshire Healthcare NHS Foundation Trust

Derek Winter DL
Deputy Chief Coroner of England and Wales and HM Senior Coroner for the City of Sunderland

Foreword

His Honour Judge Teague KC, Chief Coroner of England and Wales

In conversation with medical professionals up and down the country, I have been struck by the needless apprehension with which so many of them regard the inquest process. Many clinicians view the prospect of having to give evidence with deep trepidation, and they and their employers dread receiving a report for the prevention of future deaths. At the heart of these fears lies an understandable but misguided aversion to public criticism. But the truth is that the purpose of an inquest is not to cast blame, and a prevention of future deaths report is not a cause for shame.

The state owes a posthumous duty to the dead, as well as to those they leave behind, to investigate and record their deaths through a formal process. In England and Wales, the means by which the state discharges that duty is through the death certification system, which includes in certain cases the conduct by a coroner of a public judicial investigation known as an inquest. As the word suggests, an inquest is an inquisitorial process, the aim of which is to find out the objective truth in the public interest, and not the limited 'truth' as between and for the purposes of two or more competing interests. The coroner's inquest is the culmination of an investigative process. It is not, and should never degenerate into, a trial between combatants.

The primary responsibility for ensuring that the inquest is properly conducted is naturally that of the coroner, although lawyers who appear at inquests are bound by their own professional codes of conduct, including the legal regulators' inquest 'toolkit'. By sympathetically explaining the process to interested persons and witnesses, coroners and lawyers can do a great deal to manage expectations and thereby ensure that the inquest remains faithful to its true, inquisitorial purpose.

The calming effect of a few kindly words of reassurance should not be underestimated. A senior doctor once told me that he turned up full of foreboding at a coroner's court where he was due to give evidence but, on hearing the coroner's reminder that the process was inquisitorial and not about assigning blame, he immediately felt his nerves settle and was filled with interior peace. It is easy for legal professionals to forget that an inquest may be as daunting for medical witnesses as it is for others, including even bereaved families. At every stage of the hearing, therefore, coroners should do what they can to put interested persons and witnesses, including professional witnesses, at their ease.

Equally, hospital trusts and other organisations need to understand that the purpose of a prevention of future deaths report is not to criticise or humiliate. It is to draw attention, without recommending any specific solution, to the existence of possible learning points. That is something to welcome in the public interest, not to seek to avoid, as if it were some kind of badge of dishonour.

In recent years, coroners have done a great deal to make inquest hearings less intimidating and disruptive for all concerned, including medical professionals. Clinicians should not be required to give oral evidence at all, unless it is really necessary for them to do so. In appropriate cases, a coroner may allow a witness to give evidence remotely, but I should like to caution against the abuse of this facility. Clinicians are, of course, very busy people. They rightly assign the highest priority to the treatment of their patients, yet attendance in person at an inquest also demands high priority, for medical professionals have an integral and important role to play in the discharge of the state's posthumous duty to the dead. However great the temptation to plead pressure of work as a kind of trump card in support of an application to give evidence remotely, it should not be forgotten that the clinician's physical presence in court, perhaps making eye contact with the bereaved, can produce a remarkably powerful healing effect, perhaps even to the extent of persuading the family that everything was indeed done that could have been done. Such reconciliation is far less likely where the family see only a 'talking head' on a remote monitor. There will be some cases, therefore, in which the benefit of personal attendance will outweigh any accompanying inconvenience.

I welcome the publication of this new book. It represents an excellent initiative, and will, I am sure, provide invaluable support for professionals attending inquests.

Dame Professor Clare Gerada PRCGP FRCPsych, Past President Royal College of General Practitioners, Medical Director National Primary Care Gambling Service and Patron of Doctors in Distress

An inquest constitutes an investigation into the circumstances surrounding a person's death. Its primary objective is to ascertain the deceased individual's identity, unravel the details of how, when and where they passed away, and provide the necessary information for official death registration.

Although not a trial in the traditional sense, the atmosphere during an inquest can closely resemble that of a courtroom.

My first encounter with an inquest remains vivid in my memory. Two months into my first House Officer role, and only qualified for eight weeks, a patient under my care succumbed to internal bleeding, a consequence of complications arising from warfarin administration. Unfortunately, his bleeding time, indicated by the international normalised ratio (INR) blood test, was never assessed post-discharge. Since then, I have participated in approximately a dozen inquests, either as an interested person (an individual closely connected to the deceased or the circumstances surrounding the death) or, more recently, as an expert witness. While this may seem relatively few given my over 40 years of qualification, each instance has left an indelible mark, familiarising me with the procedural intricacies and the palpable anxiety experienced by all involved.

Being the last clinician to have interacted with a patient before their demise invariably invokes a sense of guilt. However, often, as exemplified by the man whose death resulted from a lack of testing, it is the culmination of a sequence of unfortunate errors that collectively lead to the outcome – death. Fatalities may arise from natural causes or unforeseen circumstances, underscoring the complexity inherent in the inquest process.

Inquests are serious processes, and it is essential to be well-prepared.

Inquests serve as a vital mechanism, yet regrettably, their intersection with the realm of medicine often unfolds in tragic circumstances. Despite the inherent sorrow, these moments of tragedy present an opportunity for positive transformation. Repeatedly, I've witnessed professionals seizing this opportunity to provide support to grieving families. A recent case I was involved in exemplifies this, where the coroner, recognising the delicate nature of a situation involving suicide linked to gambling addiction, exhibited remarkable care and attention throughout the inquest.

In navigating this sensitive matter, the coroner took great care to elucidate the rationale behind their final determination. This instance underscored the relational nature of the inquest process, emphasising the connection between the coroner and the bereaved. Even amid the legal and medical dimensions, the compassion demonstrated by the coroner served as a poignant reminder that, at its core, an inquest is a compassionate engagement between legal and medical professionals and those who have suffered a loss.

No one goes to work wishing to deliberately make an error or disregard issues that could lead to harm, and the role of the inquest is not to attribute blame. A common fear for the professional is vulnerability; this book will help you identify possible vulnerabilities so you can address them before the inquest. This is not a defensive move, but the essence of patient safety. We are working in challenging times, and a proactive response to patient safety issues will never be criticised.

Maintaining professionalism is essential in these circumstances, but can be difficult due to the prompted emotions. The only way to achieve this is through carefully preparing and understanding the processes. This book addresses the professional and emotional dimensions, giving practical advice to enable those giving evidence or supporting colleagues to fulfil their duty.

I would encourage all healthcare professionals to read this book; attending an inquest is always stressful; if we, as a community, can increase our collective understanding, it will support resilience within the workforce, but also afford the relatives a more significant opportunity for closure and future patients the benefit of any knowledge gained.

The Aim of This Book

Gabrielle Pendlebury and Derek Tracy

The work of coroners' courts often elicits confusion, anxiety and fear in clinicians. We have written this book for clinicians, but it is equally applicable to other professionals with a duty of care who may be called to attend an inquest. We believe that it will be of relevance and assistance to social workers, managers, governance and safety leads, counsellors, psychotherapists, probation officers, allied health professionals, nurses and doctors in primary and secondary care. The book is intended for professionals working in England and Wales;[1] we specifically cover those jurisdictions, but it is not intended as an alternative to legal advice. We would hope that future editions will cover Scotland, Northern Ireland and the Republic of Ireland.

Our motivation for writing this book arises out of our experiences of attending inquests and the impact they have had on us, both personally and professionally. We hope that by passing on our knowledge, and that of our contributors, we will aid others in understanding and negotiating this potentially complex and emotionally laden process. Further, it is our expressed hope that this will in turn assist the coroner and their court in fulfilling their duties. Too often, the coroner's court is perceived as an adversarial environment to be avoided when possible, and minimised when engagement is necessitated. It is critical for clinicians and other professionals to recognise why it is a necessary, essential and healthy part of a contemporary well-governed healthcare system. Effective engagement further assists the families and friends of the deceased to understand what has happened to their loved one, as well as helping ensure the upholding and improving of standards of care, and reducing the likelihood of recurrence of harm.

Each chapter provides basic information that we consider most helpful for understanding what is going on in a coroner's court and why, from the perspective of someone faced with the prospect of providing evidence to an inquest on behalf of their organisation or themselves. It also gives practical advice based on years of experience helping other people negotiate the process during what is often a stressful time for all those involved. By breaking down the steps and what to remember at each point, the book aims to make it easier for witnesses to go through the process with clarity and confidence.

---

[1] NHS Wales delivers services via seven health boards and three NHS Trusts (www.gov.wales/nhs-wales-health-boards-and-trusts). For simplicity, we will use Trust when referring to a health board or NHS Trust.

Chapter

1

Introduction

Gabrielle Pendlebury and Derek Tracy

People reasonably expect their healthcare professionals to avoid causing harm. In the UK, there are various clinical and governance checks and balances to ensure that the individual is safe and treated with appropriate evidence-based care, and safeguards by the state to explore and investigate when these appear to have been breached. These include internal organisational disciplinary proceedings, public complaints processes, ombudsman investigations, civil claims for compensation, and criminal prosecutions, among others. In England and Wales, the coroner's inquest is one such check and balance.

A Unique Type of Court

The coroner's court in England and Wales is distinct from civil and criminal courts. It is inquisitorial, finding facts that lead to a conclusion, as opposed to the adversarial model of criminal and civil courts that seek a verdict or compensation. In the criminal court, the judge's determinations are guilty or not guilty. Civil courts decide whether a law was broken or a duty was breached. In criminal and civil courts, questioning is usually led by a barrister (counsel). However, at an inquest, the questioning is led by the coroner, who determines what has caused a death and what has contributed, more than minimally or trivially, to that death. Imprisonment or compensation are not available outcomes and there is no punishment.

The Notifications of Deaths Regulations 2019 (Regulation 3 [1]) imposes a duty on a registered medical practitioner to notify the relevant senior coroner of a death in certain prescribed circumstances (2). About half of all deaths in the UK are reported to the coroner, but not all of these lead to an inquest. If there is no doctor able to issue a certificate of death, explaining the cause of death, then it must be reported to the coroner. There are rules governing when a doctor can issue a certificate of death, they must know what illness caused the patient's death and must have seen and treated them for that illness within the last 28 days before they died (this can include via face-to-face or video) (3). These rules are in place to safeguard patients and ensure accurate reporting and registration of death.

Even when the cause of death is known or assumed to be known, some must still always be reported to the coroner:

- death linked to medical treatment or surgery;
- death linked to an accident;
- death linked to drugs or medication, whether prescribed or illicit;
- if there is a possibility the person died by suicide;
- if there are suspicious circumstances or a history of violence towards, or from, the deceased person.

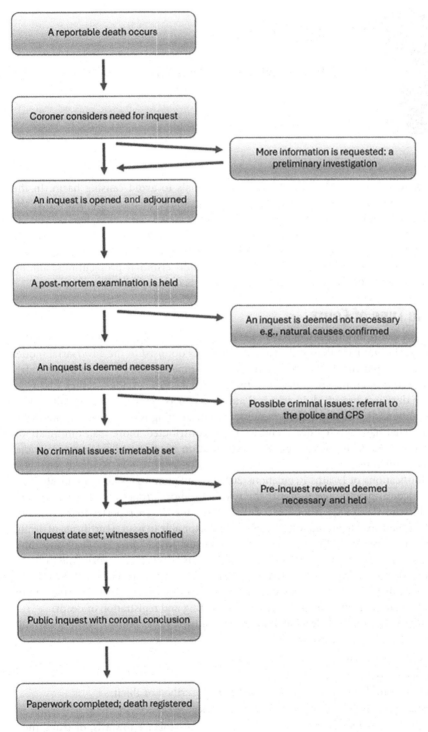

Figure 1.1 A summary of the inquest process.
Source: Crown Prosecution Service (CPS).

Box 1.1 Legislation and Statutory Instruments used by coroners (5)

Coroners and Justice Act 2009: CJA
The Coroners (Investigations) Regulations 2013: Regs
The Coroners (Inquests) Rules 2013: Rules
The Coroners Allowances, Fees and Expenses Regulations
Human Tissue Act 2004: HTA
Notification of Deaths Regulations 2019

Upon receiving such a report, the coroner's office will decide on the next steps. Within the coroner's court, there are no parties (neither defence nor prosecution as found in criminal trials, nor defendant or respondent as usual in civil cases), only 'interested persons' (4). There is no cross-examination, only questioning to elicit facts. There is no 'case' being presented.

The coroner's court also has no set 'procedural rules'. What this means is that the coroner (and not the interested persons) determines the process of investigation and hearings, the scope of the investigation and inquest, and which witnesses to call and which experts to instruct. The coroner may invite submissions from interested persons on these matters. In court, the coroner asks questions first of the witnesses and, although that may expose errors, it is essentially a neutral inquiry to establish the facts and understand decisions, actions and omissions that may have contributed to or prevented death. See Box 1.1 for a summary of the legislation and statutory instruments used by coroners.

History of the Coroner's Court

Arif Naqvi and Gabrielle Pendlebury

How the Role of the Coroner Was Established in England and Wales

The office of the coroner has a long history. In Middle English, the word coroner meant 'crown', derived from the French '*couronne*' and Latin '*corona*', and was used to refer to an officer of the Crown. The role of the coroner probably existed in Anglo-Saxon times, but it was only given something akin to statutory recognition in 1194 (6), when the 'Articles of Eyre' decreed that an office of *custos placitorum coronae* (Latin for 'keepers of the pleas of the Crown') be established.

The Eyre system was designed to protect the financial interests of the king. It required every county to elect three knights and clerks to maintain records on issues of interest to the Crown. These records allowed royal functions (including justice) to travel the whole country to handle all matters of financial interest to the king in local affairs. Under the Eyre system, 'keeping the pleas' was an administrative task assigned to the locally resident coroner, while 'holding the pleas' was a judicial one left to judges who travelled around the country holding assize courts (periodic courts held to handle the most important local cases). In effect, the coroner was the local representative of the Crown in each county.

The role of the coroner developed organically out of their responsibility to protect the king's financial interests. Coroners were required to be landed gentry (7), presumably to ensure appropriate liability for tax-collecting duties, with their possessions being used in the event of a failure of collection. The duties of early coroners included the investigation of almost any aspect of medieval life that had the potential to bring revenue to the Crown. Coroners investigated suicides because the goods and chattels of those found guilty of the then crime of '*felo de se*' (or 'self-murder') would be forfeited to the Crown, as were shipwrecks and discoveries of buried treasure. Indeed, a historical remnant is that identifying treasure troves that may belong to the State remains one of the duties of coroners today.

A key financial interest was levying a fine known as the '*murdrum*', from which the word 'murder' is derived. The fine was instituted following the Norman Conquest, after King William noticed that many of his soldiers would be found slain in outlying places and he was unable to ascertain who was responsible. To deter local communities from killing Normans, a heavy fine was therefore levied on any village where a corpse was discovered, with a presumption that the deceased was Norman, unless they could be proved to be English. The person who found a body from a death thought sudden or unnatural was required to raise a 'hue and cry' (shouting and loudly pursuing anyone they witnessed committing a crime) and to notify the coroner (8).

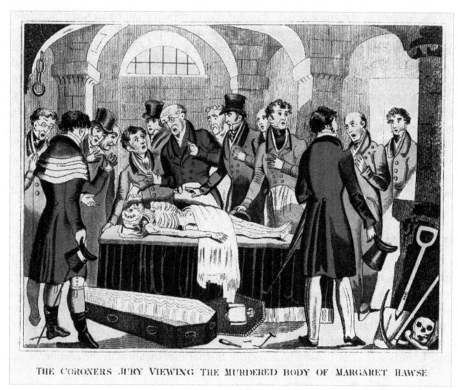

THE CORONERS JURY VIEWING THE MURDERED BODY OF MARGARET HAWSE

Figure 2.1 The coroner's jury viewing the murdered body of Margaret Hawse from John Fairburn's chapbook of 1829.
Courtesy of Bishopsgate Institute.

The coroner's jury would be summoned to participate in an inquest which had the purpose, then as now, of ascertaining the identity of the deceased and how, when and where they had died. Many early coroners' inquests dealt with the 'Presumption of Normanry' which could only be rebutted by the local community (which thus avoided a fine) by the 'Presentment of Englishry' (9). Jurors may have been able to identify the deceased and could examine the body to discover the cause of death, potentially obvious from any injuries that might be seen. Until modern times, the jury was required to view the body, and inquests were held promptly as refrigeration was not an option.

Coroners were considered the principal agents of the Crown in bringing criminals to justice (7). During the thirteenth and fourteenth centuries, before the rise of what became the justices of the peace, they were apparently responsible for preserving order. Coroners were introduced in Wales through the Statute of Rhuddlan in 1284, following the military conquest of the country by Edward I of England in 1282. The role of coroners narrowed in the sixteenth century. In this period, judicial functions were centralised in the King's Court, 'escheators' emerged and took over the coroner's financial duties, and justices of the peace took over other duties. The sole important role that coroners retained was that of holding inquests into cases of violent or unnatural deaths.

Public interest in unnatural deaths ensured that coroners retained an important role. Public concern and panic caused by inaccurate recording of the actual numbers of deaths arising from epidemics such as cholera prompted the government to pass the first Births and Deaths Registration Act in 1836. Ten years later, The Coroners' Society of England and Wales was formed by Sergeant William Payne Esq., HM Coroner for Southwark and the City of London. This coincided with concern that easy access to various poisons, alongside inadequate medical investigations into the actual causes of deaths, was leading to many homicides going undetected.

By the end of the nineteenth century, the role of the coroner had largely achieved its current shape. The Coroners Act of 1887 became the basis for modern coroner law (now framed in the Coroners Act 1988 and the Coroners Rules 1984), and in 1888, The Local Government Act finally abolished the election of coroners who were now to be appointed by local authorities.

The Medical Examiner

The Coroners and Justice Act 2009 (4) ('the Act') revised the law on coroners and criminal justice in England and Wales and created a new office: the medical examiner, who would have a defined geographical area to oversee, with national coverage. The principal purpose of the Act was to establish a more effective, transparent, and responsive justice and coroner service for victims, bereaved families and the wider public. The role of the medical examiner in this new system was to examine every death that occurs in their locality and refer those which require further investigation to the coroner.

Coroners in the Twenty-First Century

At the beginning of his appointment, the first Chief Coroner of England and Wales, Sir Peter Thornton KC, Chief Coroner 2012–2016, gave the following summary of the purpose of a twenty-first-century coroner system (10).

(1) **The need to know**
The public, especially bereaved family members and friends, need to know what happened and how the deceased came by their death. This applies particularly to deaths in custody or at the hands of an agent of the state, where there is a wider duty to protect citizens from wayward or mistaken actions by the state as well as to expose wrongdoing and bad practice. However, the public need to know applies to all deaths where there is a real element of uncertainty.

The interests of the bereaved family is [sic] at the heart of this public process, which is designed to give them answers, where that is possible. It is not a question of laying blame or apportioning guilt, either civil or criminal, as that is expressly forbidden by law. The investigation process is inquisitorial (rather than adversarial), with a view to seeking out and recording as many facts concerning the death as the public interest requires. Although it is a fact-finding exercise and not a method of apportioning guilt, the process can still find fault in someone or something. Where something has gone wrong, it can and must record how they either led directly to the death or contributed to it – for example, hospital or care home neglect – but only by giving statements of fact, not by giving an opinion or judgment. (Statements of fact can be verified or proven to be true. An opinion or judgment is based on those facts, an attempt to draw a conclusion from factual evidence. This is not within the remit of the coroner (or jury).)

A determination may not be framed in such a way as to appear to determine any question of criminal liability on the part of a named person, nor of civil liability (4).

The coroner is an independent judicial officer, with powers to summon witnesses and jurors and hear evidence under oath. They have a duty to conduct a full, fair, and fearless investigation (11). The verdict of the coroner or the jury can be in a short-form (such as 'unlawful killing', 'suicide', or 'accident', or it can be expressed in a brief, neutral, factual statement that expresses no judgment or opinion.

(2) Preventing Future Deaths
The coroner system exists to provide justice to the public not only in identifying causes of death but in preventing future deaths of a similar nature, something which families often feel passionately about. They say, and rightly say, our beloved should not have died in those circumstances, and what is more we do not want his death to be in vain; we do not want it to happen to anyone else in that same way.

Coroners are under a duty, and one which I shall emphasise, to report to Government and local government and agencies and institutions so that lessons can be learned for the future.

(3) Compassion and understanding
An understanding of the fragility of life and 'the need for compassion and understanding, and the provision of a system of fair justice for everybody, in life and in death.'

Recent Changes to the Coroner's Court

The role of the coroner has been broadened, in particular, Clauses 37 to 41 of the Judicial Review and Courts Bill (12) (the Bill), introduced in the House of Commons on 21 July 2021, deal specifically with coroners.

The Bill aims to broaden the circumstances in which a coroner might *discontinue* an investigation. If they are satisfied that the cause of death has become clear in the course of the investigation, and an inquest into the death has not yet begun, a coroner is enabled to call off the inquiry. Previously, unless the cause of death had been revealed by a post-mortem examination, once an investigation had been started, the coroner had no power to discontinue it and there had to be an inquest.

The Bill aims to give the coroner more flexibility in how they hold inquests. Specifically, it allows a coroner to decide to hold an inquest in writing, without a hearing, in specified circumstances. It also makes it possible to devise rules to allow all participants, including the coroner, to participate remotely in pre-inquest reviews and inquests. In addition, it replaces and replicates the effect of a provision in the Coronavirus Act 2020 to make it possible for coroners to hold inquests without a jury where they have reason to suspect a death has been caused by COVID-19.

Chapter 3

The Role of the Coroner

Lydia Brown

Key Points

- Do not presume that the coroner and family will have an intuitive understanding of all medical matters; ensure as a witness that your explanations are clear and simple. If the matter is complex, consider using visual aids or potentially video assistance.
- The inquest is not there to consider fault or blame against an individual or organisation.
- The coroner will use their discretion to select witnesses, set the scope of the inquiry and to decide on expert evidence.
- In certain situations, a witness statement may be read out without the need for the witness to attend (R23). This is at the discretion of the coroner; there are no set rules.

The role of the coroner is to investigate violent, unnatural or unexplained deaths, as set out in the Coroners and Justice Act of 2009 (4). The coroner is a creature of statute; the oldest Judicial office confirmed in 1194 (6), but in existence before that time to assist the Crown with the valuable and inevitable business of death.

The coroner is an Independent Judicial Officer and remains responsible to the Crown rather than the government of the day, but the practicalities are administered by the local authorities who pay for the appointed coroners and provide office and court support. Many also use the investigative abilities of the local police force, although the coroner's officers can alternatively be employed by the local authority. There is considerable divergence of individual coroners' practices, resourcing and individual discretions that can result in bafflingly different experiences for those exposed to the service.

To qualify for appointment into this judicial office, the individual must reach the basic eligibility criteria (13) of being 5 years qualified and legally experienced as either a solicitor, barrister or fellow of the Chartered Institute of Legal Executives, but gone are the days when a medical qualification was an accepted criteria and no medical knowledge is required at all. This may be a helpful insight when the coronial questioning seems possibly eclectic or even remarkably uninformed – there is no guarantee that the 'learned coroner' understands your specifically detailed branch of medicine sufficiently to question or challenge the evidence as presented. It is for the witness to explain and possibly even bring in visual aids or offer video assistance for the more challenging technical inquests.

Scope of the Inquest

The scope of any inquest should be set out at the start and is limited by the statutory framework from where the coronial duties arise. The power of the coroner to investigate deaths is wide ranging, but not limitless, and is constrained by the law to four questions (4):

Who was the person who died? How, when and where did they come about their death?

In the vast majority of cases heard, the answer to three of these questions is just a factual recording of non-contested information, readily known to all involved. It is rare that the identity of the deceased must be investigated by the coroner and tends to be a formality. As so many deaths occur in hospitals or care situations, 'when and where' is again commonly just a formality. The deceptively tricky explanation of 'how' a death occurred tends to be the focus of most inquests. It must be explained to many families grieving their loved one that the law cannot and must not try to answer the question of 'why' this had to happen; that must be left to one side however persistent the requests to explore the sometimes messy and often complex personal lives of the suddenly deceased. The inquest should find and record the facts neutrally, succinctly and without expressing any judgement or opinion.

It is often helpful to set out what the inquest process must NOT achieve, in contrast to the statutory purpose. The inquest is not a vehicle to resolve family grievances or hospital complaints, it does not consider issues of fault or blame against an individual or an organisation. It must not phrase any conclusion to appear to determine any question of criminal or civil liability, and any coronial conclusion will not impede the workings of the adversarial courts. If criminal proceedings are pending, the inquest process will be suspended and only resumed if there is 'sufficient reason' to do so after the criminal matters have been concluded. The coroner works in tandem with other statutory organisations who may be investigating deaths (such as the Care Quality Commission [CQC] and Health and Safety Executive [HSE]) to decide who should proceed first.

The investigatory process varies widely between individual deaths, from a single hearing when the inquest is opened and concluded at the same time, with no need for live witnesses and no disputed evidence. An example is a death from mesothelioma, almost always a consequence of exposure to asbestos fibres and therefore if the exposure is due to employment, classed as an unnatural death due to industrial disease. Other inquests can require days of court time, numerous witnesses and a long list of 'interested persons' (see below) who have an interest in the findings and conclusion.

The duty and responsibilities of the coroner are best described in the leading case of *Jamieson*:

> It is the duty of the coroner as the public official responsible for the conduct of inquests, whether he is sitting with a jury or without, to ensure that the relevant facts are fully, fairly and fearlessly investigated ... He must ensure that the relevant facts are exposed to public scrutiny, particularly if there is evidence of foul play, abuse or inhumanity. He fails in his duty if his investigation is superficial, slipshod or perfunctory. But the responsibility is his. He must set the bounds of the inquiry. He must rule on the procedure to be followed. (11)

While the language may seem a little archaic today, the sentiments resonate. The discretion of the coroner to select the witnesses, to set the scope of the inquiry and decide if expert evidence is required cannot be challenged unless it is unreasonable. It is not infrequent that witnesses say when contacted by the court officials that they will not be attending court, for a miscellany of reasons and excuses, but this is due to a fundamental misunderstanding of their duty to the court. The coroner has the power to summon a witness to court, and failure to present can have the consequences of arrest and even imprisonment. On rare occasions, it is necessary to utilise these statutory powers if the mere threat proves insufficient.

Rule 23

It is commonly the case that witness statements are provided and the evidence can be simply read onto the court record, without the need for the witness to attend to answer any questions. This is a procedure under Rule 23 of the Coroners Rules 2013 (14) (Chapter 10). R23 evidence can be accepted for many different reasons, including 'good and sufficient reason' why the maker of the statement should not attend. There is no list of what satisfies this criterion; this remains firmly within the discretion of the coroner. Examples of where evidence might be admitted under this provision include the witness being on maternity leave or long-term sick, no longer residing in England or Wales (the coroner powers are limited geographically) or being incarcerated, but nothing gives an automatic right of non-attendance: each case is judged on its own facts.

The Statement: A Coroner's Perspective

Preparation for an inquest by the witnesses is key to a positive outcome and the preparation needs to commence as soon as the death occurs or it is recognised that the coroner is involved. Chapter 9 will detail this process, but from a coroner's perspective, a good statement does not have to be pages long, encompassing each twist and turn of the treatment and crammed full of medical descriptions or, even worse, medical abbreviations. Remember that the coroner is unlikely to have a medical qualification and the family and legal representatives will be even less likely to be able to understand or follow this unless clear, jargon-free explanations are provided. If something was not done that should have been done, set this out clearly and unambiguously, when this was identified and how it was corrected. If there is an explanation for how it happened, provide that to the court to assist with the findings of fact; remember the court is not looking to establish fault or blame. The same approach should be adopted for things that were done in error, with an explanation and, if appropriate, acknowledgement of the consequences of the act.

Unless there has been a specific request for an overview report, avoid detailing other clinicians' involvement, in particular any perception of criticism of other individuals. If the coroner requires additional statements, they will be requested, or this should be identified by the legal advisers. It will rarely be beneficial for the surgeon to set out that it was all the fault of the anaesthetist, or the midwife to allege in a statement that the doctor should have sought senior assistance (unless this was clearly and unequivocally documented at the time). There should be adequate provision for the contents of any statement to be discussed with a legal overview for advice, but be mindful that timetables can be tight and it will only be to the detriment of the statement provider if the job is put off for so long that it has to be submitted before the Trust incurs potential penalties. The coroner has the power to require statements to be submitted under a 'Schedule 5' notice by a certain date with the threat of a fine 'not exceeding £1000 on a person who fails without reasonable excuse to do anything required'. No coroner will wish to invoke this fine, but this enforcement is in the statute for good reason, and it can and has been used as a last resort to move the investigation forward. Avoid this potentiality by early positive engagement with the process, seeking assistance and seeing this as an opportunity to explain your actions, acknowledge learning points and reflect on past and future practice.

Patient Safety Incident Response Framework: A Coroner's Perspective

A well-prepared Trust will have taken all appropriate steps to investigate the incident that led to the death, be able to demonstrate steps taken to avoid recurrence and considered and shared learning and training issues arising. There is likely to be an internal report, the patient safety incident response framework (PSIRF) taking over from the root cause analysis and Serious Incident reporting. This will be detailed in the next chapter, but from a coroner's perspective, this will be shared and discussed at the inquest. **It still happens that these reports are not shared with the clinicians, which can create a somewhat tense series of question and answer, either between the coroner and the witness, or the family/their legal representative and the witness.** It can be difficult to retain credence that lessons have been learned if the responsible clinician has no knowledge of the Trust's findings or the action plan devised to demonstrate progress. Equip yourself with not only a copy of your statement, but also the court bundle, as this should include all relevant documents and be available well in advance of the hearing. You will not feel prepared and confident if you have to scan-read several hundred pages of documents a few minutes before the hearing commences.

Giving Evidence: A Coroner's Perspective

When giving evidence, you should have received the usual advice relevant for all court appearances (see Chapters 11–14), so it may seem trite to rehearse that again. However, having spent many, many days in court presiding over hundreds of inquests, some obvious mistakes are so common they still occur with unwanted consequences. If you attend in person, check the actual court, do not make assumptions (it is frustrating to be told at 10.10am that your witness is trying to get a taxi from the Magistrates court where they went in error for a 10.00am start). Do not be late; early is fine, late demonstrates incompetence, indifference and poor planning, and can result in a humiliating apology as the first words you utter to the court. Remember you are part of a process that the family may see as their only avenue to obtain answers, move forward and speak on behalf of their loved one. It is never appropriate to be seen talking frivolously or laughing with colleagues within or near the court building as this can be interpreted as disrespectful, even if you are on another topic entirely – the family will only be thinking about their loss.

When, finally, you are asked to enter the witness box, be ready to take the oath (holy books are provided, but you may wish to bring your own: mention this to the court usher) or to affirm, and to confirm your name and occupation. Do not worry about showing some emotion. Some professional witnesses develop a close relationship to the deceased and understandably are personally upset, particularly when in such proximity to their relatives in the unfamiliar and emotionally charged court setting. Any coroner should be quietly supportive of all the attendees and extend the courtesy of a short break, a glass of water and a thoughtfully placed box of tissues. There is no problem with visible emotion in court, but for the right reasons.

Questioning can seem (and sometimes is) repetitive, with all interested parties entitled to ask their own questions of each witness. A calm, authoritative composed response, even if prefaced with 'as I told the coroner', is much more preferable than showing irritation. You should be aware that parties at an inquest, particularly families, are frequently not legally represented and may seem to ask irrelevant, bizarre or impossible-to-answer questions. It is perfectly proper to seek the assistance of the coroner as to whether the question should be answered, and to give reasons as to why an answer may not be forthcoming ('I was not working on that shift and am unable to say where the dentures ended up'). A difficult issue to seem to get right is expressing condolences to the bereaved family. A blanket instruction to each witness to start with this can seem robotic and insincere, but saying nothing about the loss can also reflect badly. The most appropriate approach many senior clinicians adopt is to mention some personal knowledge they have of the deceased, such as a conversation they recall of interests or hobbies and then to offer on behalf of the Trust a genuine sorrow. It can humanise some harrowing testimony and many times family members smile when they recognise that characteristic.

The inquest must achieve its statutory function, to answer the four questions, but also to allow independent scrutiny of events, to allow interested persons the opportunity to question witnesses and to draw attention to circumstances that may lead to further deaths, the 'prevention of future death' duty of the coroner. Some Trusts still seem to view the coroner writing a report regarding concerns that future deaths may occur as a calamitous outcome. Some are more enlightened and embrace any reports as a learning opportunity for discussion and dissemination. Good preparation at an early stage is likely to identify any such issues and they can then be rectified well in advance of the inquest being heard.

Finally, the ancient process of inquisitions into deaths continues to be a relevant and important feature of our society. We must all play our part.

> Show me the manner in which a nation cares for its dead, and I will measure with mathematical exactness, the tender mercies of its people, their loyalty to high ideals, and their regard for the laws of the land.
>
> William Ewart Gladstone (1871)

Patient Safety Incident Response Framework and Inquests

Elaine Chung, Eva Ferlez, Christopher Hilton, Shaun O'Connell and Derek Tracy

Key Points

- The PSIRF is a new mandated NHS secondary care safety and incident learning framework.
- Key improvements are a flexible proportionate approach, compassionate respectful engagement and a collaborative non-blaming improvement focus.
- Rather than prescribe investigations, it embeds responses within a broader system and just culture of data-driven systems' improvement and learning.

The Patient Safety Incident Response Framework (PSIRF) is a new NHS-mandated approach to incident reporting. This chapter provides a brief overview with the aim of allowing readers to have an initial baseline knowledge of a framework with which they will have to work in the coming years.

When a death is unexpected, the National Health Service (NHS) Trust involved has various obligations, including under the principles of duty of candour (15) and national regulations (16), and will usually conduct an investigation. This is to determine what has occurred and ensure that lessons are learned from the incident. Such an investigation can be internal to the organisation, or occasionally externally commissioned, which may be due to the complexity of the issues or merely due to limited resources for investigation.

The previous Serious Incident Framework (2015), with its thresholds for investigation and set timelines, was replaced in 2022 by a new system, envisioned to be a more flexible, improvement-focused system called the Patient Safety Incident Response Framework (17). The PSIRF applies to all services provided under the NHS standard contract, including NHS-funded services in the independent sector. It does not apply to primary care currently due to their recognised more limited internal resource; such clinicians may wish to work with their local Integrated Care Board and the other local partners to review care and management and identify learning. In other organisations offering services outside the NHS standard contract, the processes may be different as independent organisations will have developed their own governance structures to meet their specific needs. However, the objective is the same, to **implement learning to improve and maintain patient safety.** PSIRF is intended to channel resources where they will have the most impact, rather than producing repetitious incident investigation reports, with generic recommendations, which has been a broader concern about previous processes and guidelines. See Box 4.1 for a summary of the key improvements and changes with PSIRF.

Box 4.1   Key Improvements and Changes with PSIRF

Flexibility of Approach

Organisations have greater autonomy in deciding when 'patient safety incident investigation' (PSII) (19) should take place, with promotion of proportionality in a range of system-based approaches, including 'swarm huddles' (20), multidisciplinary team (MDT) reviews, after-action reviews, thematic reviews and horizon scans. PSIRF removed the 'serious incident' classification and distinctions based upon incident categories and levels of harm. PSIIs and other responses are mandatory in certain situations (21): patient deaths thought more likely than not to be due to problems in care; deaths of patients detained under the Mental Health Act; and incidents that meet the 'never events' criteria (22).

If an organisation is satisfied that risks are already being appropriately managed to redress known contributory factors, it is acceptable not to undertake an individual response to an incident (other than to engage with those affected and record that the incident occurred), but to look organisation-wide and make a collective response through an action plan. The guidance supports organisations to maximise learning and improvement rather than basing responses on more arbitrary and subjective definitions of harm. Organisations can explore patient safety incidents relevant to their context and the populations they serve rather than exploring only those that meet a certain nationally defined threshold (21).

Relevant care provider organisations[1] must comply with standards for the completion of the PSIRF, including the requirements around competencies/levels of training for those involved in delivering and leading on this. Care Quality Commission (CQC) teams will apply these PSIRF standards as part of their assessment of an organisation's systems for responding to patient safety incidents.

Engagement

'Compassionate engagement' ensures that patients, their families and staff are appropriately involved in the process. 'Engaging and involving patients, families and staff following a patient safety incident' (23) includes detailed practical advice on how to engage/involve patients, families and clinical staff right from the start and throughout the incident response.

Improvement Focus

PSIRF requires regulators of services, such as the CQC and integrated care boards (ICBs) (24), to support a coordinated cross-system approach to oversight of their services, and to consider the strength and effectiveness of providers' response processes, with incident response policies and plans approved by their ICB. A supportive collaboration cross-system approach is encouraged, with ICBs facilitating collaborative working, including representatives from different organisations joining investigations, at both place and system level, not limited by organisational boundaries (25).

In reality, without obligations on the providers of services to adhere to the ICBs, this is unlikely to happen, but we will be watching this space for the second edition of this book.

---

[1] The PSIRF is a contractual requirement under the NHS Standard Contract and as such is mandatory for services provided under that contract, including acute, ambulance, mental health and community healthcare providers. This includes maternity and all specialised services. Primary care providers may also wish to adopt PSIRF, but it is not a requirement at this stage. Further exploration is required to ensure successful implementation of the PSIRF approaches within primary care.

In addition to the learning reviews conducted and led by the healthcare providers themselves, the Health Services Safety Investigations Body established in October 2023 (replacing the Healthcare Safety Investigation Branch formed in 2017) is an independent, arms-length body of the Department of Health and Social Care able to conduct independent patient safety investigations across the NHS and healthcare settings in England (18).

It is thus likely that in the case of an unexpected death there will be more than one investigation occurring. Clinicians and other professionals might face the scenario of needing to provide statements for both an internal organisational PSIRF process and the coroner's court, and timing may mean that different information is available at different time points. While this has the risk of being confusing or onerous for the clinician, they should not defer writing their statements for court until any internal investigation is complete. However, they may reserve the right to make a supplementary statement when the report has been published, should this be required.

The coroner has powers to direct the disclosure of the interview records from the PSIRF incident investigation, mortality case reviews, audits or any other documents that may be relevant to how the death occurred. Any uncertainty about issues of confidentiality or information governance would require appropriate guidance and support from the relevant individuals and teams, such as the Trust Caldicott Guardian where available, the legal representative or your defence organisation. The Trust may propose to the coroner that the interview records from the PSIRF incident investigation are confidential, and they may be disclosed to the coroner only in confidence (*R (AP)* v. *HM Coroner Worcestershire* [26]). They usually only become potentially disclosable to 'interested persons' (Chapter 7) if there are conflicts in the evidence that require attention as part of the inquest. Before attending court, it is important to read and understand the incident review. If this highlights any issues, such as factual inaccuracies, it allows time to evaluate and prepare an explanation in advance of giving evidence, an area we explore further in future chapters.

The Principles of the PSIRF

PSIRF is *not* an investigation framework that prescribes what to investigate; instead, it:

- embeds patient safety incident response within a wider system of improvement;
- prompts a cultural shift towards systematic patient safety management; and
- advocates a coordinated and data-driven approach that prioritises compassionate engagement with those affected.

As part of this framework, coroners should be contacted at the earliest opportunity (27). There is not a uniform national system for such contact at present: some require an emailed referral form, while others accept telephone referrals, so knowing how to 'engage' with your coroner will be dependent on local practice. The PSIRF also assists the broader NHS principles of probity, sharing of information and learning from incidents. Further, it aims to remove the potential unintended barrier of coroners being unaware or uninformed of any relevant internal processes or learning. This is particularly pertinent as local processes are likely to be completed before those of the coroner's court, and thus valuable information may be available to assist the coroner.

PSIRF makes it mandatory for organisations to develop a patient safety incident response policy and a patient safety incident response plan, which must be available on the organisation's website, and based upon a review of the organisation's patient safety incidents and improvement priorities.

PSIRF does not prescribe what to investigate, with a few exceptions, and there are no prescribed timelines for investigations, with these to be agreed on a case-by-case basis (although learning responses should usually be completed within 1–3 months, and within 6 months at the latest). An early incident review will feed into the decision making and planning of further learning reviews in line with the provider's clinical processes and policies, determining issues such as: its scope and terms of reference; any required expert advice; how detailed and comprehensive the review should be; the panel and Chair, and whether internal or external to the organisation; and identification of other relevant processes, such as safeguarding reviews and coroner's inquests.

Professionals' contributions at these will vary in form, from informal group meetings to written statements. Advance notice will be given and employer support provided; one might also wish to speak to a defence organisation or union. Human errors can and do occur within complex systems; however the focus for learning and improvement should be on the work-systems, and not on the individual (28).

NHS England has created a training programme for NHS staff called the NHS Patient Safety Syllabus, with a focus on working to create a positive patient safety culture and building safer systems across all areas in the NHS. Anyone looking to learn more about patient safety systems and recognising their own role in patient safety improvement is recommended to access this training (29).

The just culture principles further ensure that learning from patient safety incidents focuses on system factors and does not single out an individual inappropriately or unfairly. Healthcare providers are required to follow the principles set out in the NHS England 'A just culture guide' (30), which is intended to: '. . . [encourage] managers to treat staff involved in a patient safety incident in a consistent, constructive and fair way'.

An NHS Trust View: Perspectives of a Chief Operating Officer

In most cases, by the time an inquest is started at the coroner's court, an organisation will have already completed a number of internal inquiries, and may have also participated in other external ones, into the circumstances around the death. This normally includes the organisation being notified of the death involving a patient, recording this, and undertaking an immediate incident or mortality review to understand if there were any acts or omissions in the care provided which may have contributed to the death. Where appropriate, external parties including commissioners and regulators are informed, and an investigation is commissioned, and areas for learning developed into an action plan.

The PSIRF emphasises that such incident reviews must ensure compassionate and meaningful involvement of those affected in both the investigation and the learning response, and that the learning should be timely and completed no longer than 6 months after the incident occurred. **Audit of the implementation of learning and the effectiveness of any changes made will no doubt be a priority for all Trusts with a focus on patient safety.**

At an inquest, Interested Persons may be invited to submit evidence specifically outlining what the organisation has learned about the incident and the action taken since to prevent recurrence. If the coroner remains concerned following the inquest that other deaths will occur, they have a duty to issue a report which any organisations named must respond to formally within 56 days, and in most circumstances the coroner's report and the response are published. Although the Prevention of Future Death report (Chapter 15) is made for the benefit of the public, it may be perceived as public criticism of systems and processes within an organisation. Therefore, there is a preference to present – candidly and in detail – evidence of actions completed. This may also be an opportunity to highlight to the coroner where the organisation may not have the power to take further actions which may be of concern, thereby reducing the need for the coroner to issue a PFD report to the organisation.

As an example, a recent case examined the circumstances related to the death of a man, killed by a patient under the care of a mental health trust. In the years between the death and the inquest, the incident had been examined by a serious incident investigation, a Safeguarding Adults Review, an Independent Homicide Inquiry and a criminal trial. This was unusual in that a long time had passed between the incident and the inquest, and that there were a number of Interested Persons due to the complexity of the case. This was also an inquest where the trust did not have a direct connection to the deceased, but the incident related to care provided to another individual (the assailant), who had to be informed that evidence was being given at the inquest which contained information which might otherwise be considered confidential.

The mental health trust provided a statement on learning and improvements made at the inquest and an Executive Director attended to give evidence. The evidence presented described the learning that had occurred since the death, including:

- revision of policies and protocols regarding managing transitions between services and examples of electronic tools to monitor performance;
- revision of policies and protocols regarding management of patients' medication, approaches to disengagement from care and co-existing substance misuse, and examples of changes to the electronic patient record system with audit of implementations; and
- improvement in staffing levels, supported by evidence regarding national best practices with ongoing monitoring.

The inquest found that errors, omissions or failures on the part of the Trust caused or contributed to the death, but a Regulation 28 Prevention of Future Deaths report was not issued to the Trust as the action plan and ensuing audit completed by the Trust remedied these areas.

As either a clinician or Board director, participation in an inquest process can trigger a number of emotions. It is enormously sad and distressing to examine in detail an unexpected death. As clinicians, we should always want to provide the best care that we can, and in a Board role there should always be the aspiration that our organisations deliver care that is safe and effective, while acknowledging that not every risk can be fully mitigated. The inquest does serve as a crucial checkpoint to ensure that organisations are examined around fully completing and evidencing their internal action plans, and it gives an important additional opportunity for loved ones of the deceased to ask the important

---

Box 4.2   A Trust PSIRF Investigator's Perspective

- This investigation is not to find out about, or comment on, the cause of the death; this is the coroner's role. Be mindful that you may be called to give evidence at the inquest; contact and liaise early with the legal representative if this is a possibility.
- Liaise early with the governance team so that they can support and advise on the structure of the investigation.
- The investigation can take a long time and be highly emotional; it is often a careful balancing act, holding a line between being investigator and not stepping into a pastoral role for families and clinicians.
- It is an opportunity to look at the pathway of care provided to the patient and whether anything can be learned. The aim is to identify good practice and areas for development, and make recommendations that can improve future care.
- Investigators may consider if there was a one-off lapse in normal standards or a system error that was waiting to happen due to an accumulation of factors.
- Ensure that previous investigations (and possibly complaints, claims and so forth) are considered together when preparing evidence.
- Support the court and other parties to understand the roles and remits of the organisations involved, and whether the organisation has the power to act upon PFD recommendations or if these may be more effective if addressed to another person. Always consider confidentiality issues of all involved, not just the deceased.

---

questions about 'why' a tragedy occurred and how it might be prevented from happening again. It also is important to have a chance to offer an apology. Receiving a PFD report is not a punishment for an organisation, but an important additional layer of scrutiny, which might highlight to an organisation that their own review may not have identified and adequately addressed the areas that the coroner feels are most pertinent. See Box 4.2 for a Trust PSIRF investigator's perspective.

Notification of Deaths to the Coroner and the Decision to Investigate
When to and Who Should Contact the Coroner

Karen Hall and Gabrielle Pendlebury

Key Points

- Medical practitioners have a statutory duty to notify the coroner, where the doctor suspects a 'notifiable cause' of death and where one considers a death 'suspicious', the police must also be informed immediately.
- The duties of the medical examiner.
- The duty of the coroner to investigate.

The Responsibility of Medical Practitioners to Notify the Coroner

The process of notifying deaths to the relevant authorities is a critical part of a modern healthcare system, ensuring that any deaths that may require further investigation are appropriately assessed, relevant learning is extracted and disseminated, and governance systems amended as required. **Anyone who is concerned about the cause of a death can inform a coroner about it, but in most cases a death will be reported to the coroner by a doctor or the police.** Guidance from the Ministry of Justice (31) highlights the importance of individuals notifying the coroner even if other reports or notifications have been made, and emphasises the responsibility of medical practitioners to provide relevant and accurate information to assist the court to fulfil its duties.

Medical practitioners have a statutory duty to notify the coroner (section 3(1) of the Notification of Deaths Regulations 2019 [SI 2019 No. 1112]) (1) where the doctor suspects a 'notifiable cause' of death. Prior to the updated legislation of 2019, it would generally be the registrar or a police officer who would notify the coroner of a death in the community. Now, wherever a notifiable death has occurred of which a doctor is aware, that death must also be reported directly to the coroner by a medical practitioner. **Note that where one considers a death 'suspicious', the police must also be informed immediately, and this responsibility is not to be left to the coroner.**

Ordinarily, when an individual dies, if the circumstances noted below are met, the attending medical practitioner (AMP) who is responsible for completing the medical certificate of the cause of death (MCCD) will report the death to the coroner. In addition, *any* doctor who now becomes aware of a death must notify the coroner if either: (1) there is no attending medical practitioner required to sign an MCCD or (2) the doctor who would otherwise sign the MCCD is not available to do so within a reasonable time (unless, of course, another doctor has already made the notification). The information provided in the notification helps the coroner decide whether further investigation is necessary or if the medical practitioner can issue an MCCD directly.

As of April 2024,[1] a medical practitioner is eligible to be an attending practitioner and complete an MCCD if they have attended the deceased in their lifetime. The attending practitioner will propose a cause of death, if they can do so, to the best of their knowledge and belief. Medical examiners will provide independent scrutiny of all deaths that are not referred to the coroner.

This is a simplification of previous rules that enabled medical practitioners to be an attending practitioner, to complete an MCCD, if they had attended the patient during their last illness, but required referral of the case to a coroner for review if they had not done so within the 28 days prior to death or had not seen in person the patient after death. At the time of writing this chapter, the guidance in this area had not been updated,[2] but it is likely to have been completed by publication. We therefore advise readers to review the relevant guidance for further information.

Circumstances Requiring Notification of Death to the Coroner

The coroner has some discretion as to whether an inquest should be held. However, Box 5.1 illustrates a legal ruling that highlighted how such discretion is not absolute. The following circumstances, or their suspicion, surrounding a death place an obligation on a medical practitioner to notify the coroner (1):

- **Poisoning**: deaths caused by deliberate or accidental intake of poison, including otherwise benign substances like sodium (salt).
- **Exposure to toxic substances**: deaths resulting from exposure to toxic substances, such as toxic materials, radioactive materials and so forth.
- **Medicinal products or drugs**: deaths caused by deliberate or accidental intake of medicinal products, controlled drugs, or psychoactive substances, or any complications arising from those should be notified.
- **Violence, trauma or injury**: deaths resulting from violence, trauma or injuries inflicted by others or by the deceased themselves, including accidents like falls or road traffic collisions.
- **Self-harm**: deaths reasonably suspected to be the result of poisoning, trauma or injuries inflicted by the deceased themselves.
- **Neglect**: deaths resulting from neglect, where a dependent person is not provided with basic necessities like nourishment, shelter or medical care. This includes deaths resulting from human failure, whether by acts or omissions.

---

[1] www.gov.uk/government/publications/changes-to-the-death-certification-process/an-overview-of-the-death-certification-reforms

[2] www.gov.uk/government/publications/guidance-notes-for-completing-a-medical-certificate-of-cause-of-death/guidance-for-doctors-completing-medical-certificates-of-cause-of-death-in-england-and-wales-accessible-version#referring-deaths-to-the-coroner

Box 5.1 Discretion to Hold an Inquest

R (Linnane) v. *HM Coroner for Inner North London* (32) dealt with the issue of mandatory inquests and the scope of coroners' powers. The case involved the death of James Linnane, who died while in police custody. His family sought an inquest into the circumstances surrounding his death. However, the coroner refused to hold an inquest, citing that an inquest was not mandatory under the Coroners Act 1988.

The central issue in the case was whether the coroner had a duty to hold an inquest in cases of deaths that occurred while the deceased was in the custody of the police or other state authorities. The question was whether such deaths automatically triggered a mandatory inquest. The case also raised questions about the scope of a coroner's powers and the extent to which they could exercise discretion in deciding whether to hold an inquest.

The family of the deceased argued that an inquest was mandatory under the common law principle that deaths in custody required thorough investigation to ensure transparency and accountability. The coroner put forward that the Coroners Act 1988 provided him with the discretion to decide whether an inquest was necessary, and he did not believe it was required in this case.

Judgement

The court held that there is a presumption that an inquest should be held in cases where the deceased died in the custody of the police or other state authorities. The presumption is based on the need for a thorough investigation to ascertain the cause of death and to address any concerns about the conduct of those in authority.

While the court recognised that a coroner has a certain level of discretion in deciding whether to hold an inquest, this discretion is not absolute. The coroner must give due consideration to the circumstances of each case and, in particular, the public interest in holding an inquest for deaths in custody. The coroner's discretion is limited, and it would only be appropriate to forgo an inquest in exceptional circumstances where the cause of death is clear and there are no outstanding issues that warrant investigation.

The court emphasised that the right to life under Article 2 of the European Convention on Human Rights required an effective and independent investigation into deaths in custody. This obligation supported the presumption in favour of holding an inquest.

- **Medical or similar procedures**: deaths related to medical or similar procedures, including errors made during procedures or treatment.
- **Employment-related injury or disease**: deaths resulting from injuries sustained during employment or diseases contracted during employment, such as industrial diseases.
- **Unnatural or of unknown cause**: deaths that are unnatural or of unknown cause.
- **Unknown identity of the deceased**: if the identity of the deceased is unknown.
- **Person died while in custody or otherwise in state detention**: A person is in state detention if he or she is compulsorily detained by a public authority within the meaning of section 6 of the Human Rights Act 1998 (CJA 2009, section 48(2) [4]). This is of particular relevance to psychiatrists, as state detention includes the deaths of patients detained under the Mental Health Act 1983.

The Notification Process

There are a number of formalities to be followed in order to notify the coroner correctly:

- **Timeframe:** Notifications should be made as soon as reasonably practicable after determining that notification is necessary. For suspicious deaths, the police should also be informed immediately.
- **Methods**: Notifications can be provided in writing (including through electronic methods such as email or online web portal or form where these are available) or, in exceptional circumstances, orally.
- **Written confirmation**: After an oral notification, a written notification, confirming the information provided orally, should be provided to the coroner as soon as reasonably practicable.
- **Required information**: The notification must include the registered medical practitioner's full name, address and email, the deceased's full personal details, including their occupation, the next of kin's details, the circumstances triggering notification, the place and time of death, the name of any consultant medical practitioner who attended the deceased person in the last 14 days, and any other relevant information.
- **Clear documentation**: In cases where a coroner decides that an investigation is not necessary, a 100A form will be issued by the coroner, or the case will be referred back to the medical practitioner to issue the MCCD. Clear documentation of the process should be made in the patient's notes, whether written or electronic.

In practice, in larger healthcare organisations, there will often be a team or staff member with the role of notifying the coroner, and this responsibility may not fall on the doctor in the first instance. However, if there is any uncertainty on this, the doctor must satisfy themselves that such a process exists and that relevant notification has occurred.

Medical Examiners

The Shipman Inquiry identified a weakness in the death certification system (see Box 5.2). A certificate of death showing a 'natural cause' could be registered by the registrar of deaths, without further inquiry, such as referral to the coroner. If the deceased was due to be cremated, there would be a check by the cremation referee, but if the deceased was due to be buried, there would be no further formalities.

The Coroners and Justice Act 2009 ('the Act') created a new office, medical examiner. Medical examiners have the legal role of advising medical practitioners on certification and notification to the coroner (33). When a death occurs in the community, the first time the practitioner hears of this may be from the coroner.

The duties of the medical examiner include (33):

- providing medical advice to attending medical practitioners where the cause of death is apparently natural but not clear;
- carrying out independent scrutiny of the circumstances of death to ensure the right cases are referred to the coroner;
- discussing the death with relatives of the deceased so that they can raise any concerns;
- providing general medical advice to coroners about specific cases;
- confirming the medical cause of death in all cases not investigated by a coroner;

Box 5.2 Shipman: Historical Aspects

Dr Harold Frederick Shipman, Jr. (14 January 1946–13 January 2004) was an English general practitioner and serial killer with an estimated 250 victims (34).

Dr Shipman first came to the attention of the regulator (General Medical Council) when he was treated for a Pethidine addiction and depression in the 1970s following conviction on eight charges, including obtaining pethidine by deception, forging prescriptions and unlawful possession of pethidine. A further seventy-four offences were also taken into consideration. The conviction led to his suspension from the register by the GMC and he agreed a voluntary undertaking not to return to general practice. At that time, the Home Secretary under the Misuse of Drugs Act 1971 had the power under the Act to prohibit a doctor from having controlled drugs in his or her possession. However, no such direction was made based on the police view that no patients had come to harm (now believed to be incorrect) and on the GMC's decision not to take disciplinary proceedings further.

Dr Shipman did not keep his voluntary commitment with regard to general practice and in 1977 he joined a group general practice. In 1992, he became a single-handed practitioner. It is estimated that he killed eight to ten patients per year as a member of the group practice, but this escalated to at least thirty-two in 1997, while a single-handed GP.

- reporting any serious concerns in respect of clinical governance, patient safety or public health surveillance in accordance with local reporting arrangements; and
- identifying training needs of registered medical practitioners in relation to death certification, and promoting and facilitating such training.

Duty of Coroner to Investigate

Sections 1 and 2 of the CJA 2009 are shown in Box 5.3. The Act contemplates three discrete phases in the coronial process:

1. preliminary inquiries (before formally opening an investigation);
2. an investigation (with or without an inquest); and
3. an inquest.

The first phase is to identify if the coroner has a duty to investigate. Most notifications to a coroner do not get beyond this stage, as usually an investigation is deemed unnecessary.

The preliminary inquiry will establish that the body lies within the coroner's jurisdiction and whether an MCCD can be obtained that records the death as 'natural'. If the coroner is satisfied, a Form A is issued to the registrar.

Box 5.3 Coroners and Justice Act 2009 (CJA), sections 1 and 2

(1) A senior (2) coroner who is made aware that the body of a deceased person is within that coroner's area must as soon as practicable conduct an investigation into the person's death if subsection (2) applies.

(2) This subsection applies if the coroner has reason to suspect that

    (a) the deceased died a violent or unnatural death,

    (b) the cause of death is unknown, or

    (c) the deceased died while in custody or otherwise in state detention.

In cases of 'unnatural deaths', the CJA 2009 does not provide a definition of natural or unnatural. A natural death could be assumed to be one that relates to an internal bodily event that is not influenced by external occurrences, for example, death from a myocardial infarction at home. Examples of unnatural deaths would be a delay in the diagnosis of septicaemia (35) or a young man who died following an asthmatic attack, but would have survived if the ambulance had arrived on time (36). This means that medical practitioners should advise coroners of the meaning of the MCCD and whether it relates to an intervention. Circumstances may mean that a scientifically natural death is regarded as unnatural (37) or a scientifically unnatural death is legally ruled natural (38), as demonstrated in the cases outlined in Boxes 5.4 and 5.5.

Box 5.4 Example of Where a Scientifically Natural Death Is Regarded as Unnatural
R (Touche) v. *Inner North London Coroner* (37)

On 6 February 1999 Laura Touche gave birth to twins, delivered by caesarean section. On 15 February 1999, tragically, she died. She died from a cerebral haemorrhage, the result of severe hypertension, possibly secondary to eclampsia. The medical evidence suggests that had her blood pressure been monitored in the immediate post-operative phase her death would probably have been avoided.

The critical issue raised in these proceedings is whether such a death is natural or unnatural whether, in particular, an inquest must be held into it pursuant to s.8(1) of the Coroner's Act 1988 which requires such an inquest 'where there is reasonable cause to suspect that the deceased has died an unnatural death'.

It was the coroner's contention that Mrs Touche died a natural death. Her husband contended the contrary. The Divisional Court (Kennedy LJ and Morrison J) on 22 June 2000 accepted Mr Touche's argument and directed that an inquest be held. This decision was upheld at appeal.

Box 5.5 Example of where a scientifically unnatural death is legally ruled natural: *R* v. *HM Coroner for Birmingham and Solihull ex parte Benton* (38)

R v HM Coroner for Birmingham ex parte Benton clarified the meaning of the conclusion of 'natural causes' in the context of an admission to hospital (as distinct from accident or misadventure) as follows, emphasising that such a conclusion does not equate to a finding that there have been no errors in the medical management (38):

- Where the patient was suffering from a potentially fatal condition, and the medical intervention (even if wrongly given) merely failed to prevent the death, the proper conclusion was 'natural causes' as it was the underlying condition which had caused the death.
- If there was a failure to give medical treatment to such a patient, even negligently, this would still amount to a death from natural causes.
- If the patient was suffering from a condition which was not life-threatening, but the treatment (for whatever reason) caused death, the proper conclusion was accident or misadventure, unless there was a question of unlawful killing.

Post-Mortem Examinations

A post-mortem examination is often needed to secure an MCCD and if the coroner is satisfied that there is no duty to investigate, he or she then issues a Form B to the registrar. A common, time-sensitive reason for communication with the coroner's office about post-mortem examinations is the issue of organ and tissue donation. Box 5.6 outlines this process.

Box 5.6 Example of a Service with Close Liaison with the Coroner

One service that is in constant communication with the coroner is NHS Blood and Transplant Organ Donation and Tissue Donation service. They undertake assessment of deceased patients for the possibility of tissue donation to be used in clinical transplant (eye donation for cornea transplant, heart valves, bone, tendons, femoral arteries, skin and bespoke tissue grafts) and clinical research. If a patient is suitable for donation on initial assessment, the family or designated next of kin will be approached regarding tissue donation and the evidence of decision to donate that is available via Organ Donor Registration will be presented if applicable or donation will be explored using Legislation Deemed Consent (opt out law). All organ and tissue donation is governed by the Human Tissue Act 2004. Potential donors may be referred to tissue donation from any medical professional, families, the coroner and police and for people who have died in any location or circumstances of death.

Regarding donation after death, eye donation must be completed within 24 hours of death; other tissues as above must be retrieved within 48 hours of death. In terms of organ donation, a specialist nurse will seek coronial consent for organ retrieval; they may have up to several days to complete that process depending on the location and state of the potential donor versus the brief timescales for tissue donation. Many of our donors will die in a hospital or hospice setting, in which case we will be able to ascertain a good medical history, circumstances of admission, diagnosis, treatments and a proposed cause of death. There are occasions when we receive a referral from a family member when clinical information cannot be gained or on rare occasions when a death is suspicious or traumatic when a patient has died on scene and referred by a family liaison officer in the police where no history is available.

In order to confirm suitability for tissue donation, a detailed Medical and Social History Questionnaire and legal consent paperwork will be completed with the next of kin via telephone, with all conversations being voice recorded. Once donation has been consented, the place of death or the medical practitioner will be contacted for proposed cause of death; during normal working hours, this will be discussed by the doctor and the medical examiner to determine if cause of death is agreed upon or a referral coroner is required. This process can take up to several days.

Tissue donation has a critical time in which donation post death can be pursued. For example, in the case of eye donation, a blood sample – for virology testing to support the safety of transplant – needs to occur within 24 hours of the time of death. All other tissue donation retrieval can take place up to 48 hours post death – the blood sample time constraint remains at 24 hours. Time constraints limit the opportunity to wait for an MCCD to be issued or for a decision from the medical examiner on whether a referral to the coroner is required, therefore the NHS Blood and Transplant Organ Donation and Tissue Donation service will contact the coroner's office directly to discuss the medical case and circumstances of death with the coroner or coroner's officer to gain lack of objection for tissue donation to proceed prior to a post-mortem being carried out if necessary.

Once an investigation (phase 2) is launched, it does not necessarily continue to an inquest. The coroner must discontinue the investigation if the post-mortem examination reveals a natural cause of death, and the coroner thinks it unnecessary to continue the investigation. If, however, the death is deemed an unnatural death or a violent death, or it occurred in state detention, the investigation must continue (4). The coroner may also resume an investigation they previously discontinued if new information about the death is presented.

Notification of Deaths from COVID-19

COVID-19 as a cause of death (or contributory cause) is not reason on its own to refer a death to a coroner under the CJA 2009. COVID-19 being a notifiable disease under the Health Protection (Notification) Regulations 2010, to Public Health England, does not mean a referral to a coroner is required by virtue of its notifiable status. Section 30 of the Coronavirus Act 2020 removes the requirement for a jury inquest to be held in COVID-19 cases, but does not remove the need in certain cases to establish whether it is a work-related death.

Section 1 of the CJA 2009 requires coroners to open an inquest even in the event of a natural death in state detention (such as being detained under a section of the Mental Health Act), although there is no necessary requirement to have an inquest with a jury when the death is from natural causes (section 7(2)(a) of the CJA 2009). This was confirmed by the Judicial Review and Courts Bill, which replaced and replicated the effect of a provision in the Coronavirus Act 2020 to provide that COVID-19 is not a notifiable disease for the purposes of the requirement for the coroner to sit with a jury. This enables coroners to hold inquests without a jury where they have reason to suspect a death has been caused by COVID-19.

Chapter

6

The Scope of the Investigation

Gabrielle Pendlebury and Carol Seymour

Key Points

- The purpose of an inquest is to determine the four statutory questions: who, when, where and how.
- Understanding the differences between a traditional inquest ('Jamieson Inquest' or 'Non-Article 2 Inquest') and an Article 2 inquest (also known as a 'Middleton Inquest').
- Knowing the 'short-form' and narrative conclusions available to the coroner.
- Appreciating when a jury is required.

The coroner's aim in undertaking an inquest is to determine what caused the death and what has contributed more than minimally or trivially to that death. This contrasts with a criminal case, in which the judge must determine if the defendant is guilty or not guilty, and a civil case, where it must be determined whether a specific law has been broken or a duty breached. Understanding the scope of a coroner's investigation into a death is essential, as it prevents misconceptions about the roles of the coroner and the inquest. It will govern which statements will be read, which witnesses are called and the questions that may be asked of them. This can be a complex legal area to fully understand. This chapter will lay out and explain the main areas, although the reader may find some elements are not necessary for their full engagement with the court.

The purpose of an inquest is to find out the answers to the statutory questions within the period of time that is determined relevant by the coroner. It is a fact-finding process that is inquisitorial and not adversarial, and which has no mandate to determine criminal or civil liability. In fact, an inquest is not permitted to determine or appear to determine criminal liability by a named person or civil liability (4). It is exclusively about what happened, not who was responsible for what happened. Those are matters over which the civil and criminal courts have jurisdiction.

There are four statutory questions (who, when, where and how) (4) which the law asks the investigation to try to determine:

1. **Who was the deceased?**

   The identification of the deceased person is made on the available evidence, by the name that the person was known at the time of death. In English law, you are *who you and others say you are*. In some legal systems, you are registered at birth with a name you cannot change or is difficult to change, but in English law, if you wish to change your name, you change it and then provide evidence of the change, hence the 'deed poll'.

2. **When did the death occur?**
   The circumstances of a death can make it difficult to determine the date and time of death. A drowning in a river or a death in a moving vehicle, for example, may lead to uncertainty as to the exact time of death. If this is the case, the finding will be that the body was found dead at a particular time.
3. **Where did the death occur?**
   It may be difficult to ascertain the location of death when there is doubt about the time of death. The evidence will seek to establish the possible place of death, but, if this is not possible, the finding will be that the body was found dead at a specific place.
4. **How did the death occur?**
   The most difficult question to answer is often the medical cause of death or the events leading to it, 'by what means the person came by their death' (11). This is also the question that is usually of most interest to all involved in the inquest. The question of how the deceased came by his or her death is wider than the medical cause of death alone, as it can lead the coroner to inquire into wider acts or omissions which may be directly responsible for the death occurring.

When a clinician has the opportunity to prevent death from an established illness, disease or injury, but the person dies, it may be necessary to investigate the steps taken by that clinician. The coroner may need to evaluate and rule on the actions taken before the death. The use or not of expert evidence may influence the direction of the inquiry. The coroner will use their discretion to decide on the breadth of the inquiry and may choose to admit evidence that is of relevance to preventing future deaths, even if it is of marginal relevance to the circumstances of the specific death in question. The coroner can make a PDF report even where the matter had no impact on the death in question but where highlighting the matter would be of wider benefit.

Types of Inquests

Inquests fall into two types. The first is a traditional inquest (also known as a 'Jamieson Inquest' or 'Non-Article 2 Inquest'); the second is an Article 2 inquest (also known as a 'Middleton Inquest'), which occurs in specific instances, including while an individual is held under the protection of the state or killed by an agent of the state, or if state or system policy may have contributed to the death.

A Traditional Inquest

A traditional (Jamieson/Non-Article 2) inquest can reach one of the following thirteen conclusions. The first twelve are known as short-form conclusions (Box 6.1).

Narrative Conclusions

A narrative verdict may be given in order to expand on the conclusion and to give a longer explanation of what the important issues are. This may be given instead of, or in addition to, one of the conclusions listed above.

Neglect is not a verdict in itself, but 'a rider' to another conclusion. It can be used to qualify a verdict to explain that neglect was a contributory factor. For example, a conclusion can be reached of 'accident contributed to by neglect'.

Box 6.1   The Twelve Short-Form Conclusions Available to the Coroner in a Traditional Inquest

1. Suicide
   A conclusion of suicide can only be reached where it is found that a person has voluntarily done an act for the conscious purpose of killing themselves.
2. Unlawful killing
   A conclusion of unlawful killing can essentially be returned in two circumstances:

   (i)   as a result of an unlawful act, such as an assault or murder; or
   (ii)   through gross negligence manslaughter.

3. Accident
   A conclusion of accident can be reached where deaths are truly 'accidental' in the sense that neither the acts causing death nor the consequences of those acts were intended.
4. Misadventure
   A conclusion of misadventure can be reached where someone dies as an unintended result of actions that were themselves deliberate. For example, taking prescription medication which had an unintended outcome of causing the death of the deceased.
5. Alcohol related
6. Drug related
   An accidental death resulting from abuse of alcohol or drugs or from the result of being addicted to alcohol or drugs.
7. Industrial disease
   When the death resulted from a disease caused by work; for example, mesothelioma.
8. Lawful killing
   A death is lawful in certain circumstances, such as acts of war and self-defence.
9. Natural causes
   This conclusion can be reached where, although it was initially thought that the death might be an unnatural death requiring an inquest, on further investigation it became apparent that the cause of death was a natural illness.
10. Open
    An open conclusion will be reached where there is not enough evidence to reach any other conclusion.
11. Road Traffic Accident
    A death occurring as part of a road traffic collision.
12. Stillborn
    A stillborn child is one which has issued forth from its mother after the 24th week of pregnancy and which did not at any time after being completely expelled from its mother breathe or show any other signs of life (38). Before 24 weeks is considered a miscarriage and not within the remit of the coroner.

An Article 2 Inquest

The second type of inquest is an Article 2 inquest (also known as a 'Middleton Inquest'). It is named after Article 2 of the European Convention on Human Rights (ECHR), which states:

1.   Everyone's right to life shall be protected by law. No one shall be deprived of his life intentionally save in the execution of a sentence of a court following his conviction of a crime for which this penalty is provided by law.

2. Deprivation of life shall not be regarded as inflicted in contravention of this article when it results from the use of force which is no more than absolutely necessary: (a) in defence of any person from unlawful violence; (b) in order to effect a lawful arrest or to prevent the escape of a person lawfully detained; (c) in action lawfully taken for the purpose of quelling a riot or insurrection.

The same twelve short-form conclusions, and a narrative outcome, are also available in this instance, but it is undertaken in different circumstances. It applies any time a person dies while under the care or protection of the state, such as while in an immigration centre, in prison or in police custody, or while detained (sectioned) under the Mental Health Act (*Savage* v. *South Essex Partnership NHS Trust* [39]), or if a person is killed by an agent of the state (see the box summarising the Ian Tomlinson case). An Article 2 inquest might also be held if a state policy or system failure contributed to a death (e.g. unsafe hospital policies or in certain circumstances the death of an informal mental health patient) (40). Of note, Article 2 is no longer engaged when a person dies whose deprivation of liberty has been authorised under Deprivation of Liberty Safeguards (DoLS).

A 'traditional', non-Article 2 inquest will look at when, where and how a person died, whereas an Article 2 inquest also looks at the wider circumstances surrounding a person's death and is sometimes called 'an enhanced investigation'.

Such an inquest can be more detailed and may consider issues which would otherwise be deemed to fall outside of the scope of a non-Article 2 inquest. The investigation may be considered to act like a funnel, looking at a wide range of matters, perhaps initially to allay suspicion or rumour, and then narrowing its scope to focus on elements that are causative to the death.

An enhanced investigation is required if it is argued that the UK's substantive obligation to protect the right to life has been breached. Article 2 of the European Convention on Human Rights is invoked because when the state detains someone, the state then assumes a duty to ensure that a person's right to life is protected and kept safe. See Boxes 6.2 and 6.3 for more information about enhanced investigations.

Box 6.2 Enhanced Investigation in the Ian Tomlinson Case

Below is an excerpt from an article by R. S. Bray in the *Journal of Law and Medicine* summarising the Ian Tomlinson case, which was subject to an enhanced investigation.

On 1 April 2009, 47-year-old London newspaper vendor Ian Tomlinson collapsed and died during the G20 protests in central London. The initial autopsy found death consistent with 'natural causes'. However, that finding was disputed after the public release of mobile phone video footage showing a police officer striking and pushing Tomlinson to the ground. The release of this footage changed the course of events in the case: further post-mortem examinations found blunt force trauma to Tomlinson's body; the Independent Police Complaints Commission launched a criminal investigation; and a coronial inquest opened that was presided over by public order policing expert Judge Peter Thornton QC. On 3 May 2011, a coronial jury delivered a verdict of 'unlawful killing', finding police actions against Tomlinson 'excessive and unreasonable'. The Crown Prosecution Service then revised its decision not to prosecute the officer filmed striking and pushing Tomlinson, and on 19 July 2012 the officer was acquitted of manslaughter (42).

Box 6.3 Article 2 of the ECHR

Article 2 of the ECHR provides for the right to life. As noted by the Court at [30] (43), Article 2 gives rise to separate duties on states and those exercising state duties:

1. The negative duty, to refrain from taking life without justification.
The positive duty, which includes:

   - The **framework duty**, to put in place a legislative and administrative framework to protect the right to life – in a healthcare context this includes having effective administrative and regulatory systems in place.
   - The positive **operational duty**, to take positive measures to protect an individual whose life is at risk in certain circumstances.

2. The enhanced investigative duty (**procedural duty**); this duty is 'parasitic on the possibility of a breach by a state agent of one of the substantive operational or systems duties' and requires there to be an effective public investigation by an independent official body.

There are certain minimum requirements the investigation has to meet, which are that the inquest should: be independent, effective and reasonably prompt; involve a sufficient element of public scrutiny; and involve the next of kin to the extent necessary.

Engagement of Article 2 of the EHCR, Leading to an Enhanced Investigation

Despite seemingly straightforward criteria, in practice, whether an inquest engages Article 2 involves complex analysis of case law, which determines how to judge if there is an arguable breach of the operational or framework duty.

Deaths in prison (or in hospital while still a prisoner) and in police custody engage the procedural duty automatically (44). The death of a psychiatric patient detained under the Mental Health Act will also engage Article 2, but not the death of a patient on a community treatment order (CTO). The threshold for engagement for deaths in hospital of non-detained patients is high; in other words, this seldom occurs for such 'informal' patients (45).

The threshold will only be met where an informal mental health patient is deemed to have been sufficiently vulnerable, at real and immediate risk of suicide, and that the hospital knew or ought to have known this. Here, the hospital is obliged to take reasonable steps to prevent the suicide (45). However, these points are clearly open to varying clinical interpretation, not least what is meant by, or qualifies as, 'real and immediate risk of suicide'. For example, Melanie Rabone was an informal psychiatric patient who died on home leave, having been assessed as at high risk of a future suicide attempt. It was successfully argued that the hospital had not taken reasonable steps to prevent suicide (41). Translated into the context of an inquest, this means that in such a case, the operational duty of Article 2 of the ECHR engages and the hearing must look into the broad circumstances of the death. This broad area is clearly one that will feel of relevance and potential concern to clinicians working in inpatient mental health settings, not least due to the lack of firm, objective criteria. We can only suggest that it emphasises the need for good local policies and training on clinical assessments and record keeping. Of note, this operational duty is not a category exercise applying to all patients regardless of their circumstances (46).

It is worth highlighting here the differences in relation to physically ill people with regard to Article 2 (45):

> As regards the voluntary psychiatric patient who is at risk of suicide and the patient suffering from a life-threatening physical illness who is in an 'ordinary' hospital setting, the nature of the risk to which these two categories of patient are exposed is very different. In the case of the suicide of a psychiatric patient, the likelihood is that, given the patient's mental disorder, her capacity to make a rational decision to end her life will be to some degree impaired ... Melanie was admitted to hospital because she was suffering from a mental disorder and had attempted to commit suicide. The very reason why she was admitted was because there was a risk that she would commit suicide from which she needed to be protected. On the other hand, the patient who undergoes surgery will have accepted the risk of death on the basis of informed consent. She may choose to avoid the risk by deciding not to go ahead with the medical treatment.

For readers interested in exploring this area further, *R (on the application of Maguire) (Appellant)* v. *His Majesty's Senior Coroner for Blackpool & Fylde and another (Respondents)* (47) will be of interest. This case confirms that the threshold for an arguable breach of Article 2 in healthcare settings remains high (47).

Healthcare professionals are particularly interested in Article 2 inquests that arise in relation to acts or omissions by clinicians. These only occur in 'very exceptional circumstances' where the following four components are **all** present:

1. acts or omissions by healthcare professionals must go beyond mere error or medical negligence and would need to involve denying a patient emergency treatment despite knowing that the patient's life is at risk if treatment is not given;
2. the dysfunction in question must be objectively/genuinely identifiable as systemic/ structural in order to be attributable to the state – for example, not just individual instances of something 'going wrong' or 'functioning badly';
3. the dysfunction must be causative of the harm to the patient; and
4. the dysfunction must have resulted from a failure of the state to meet its obligation to provide an effectively functioning regulatory framework (45).

Is a Jury Required?

It can often be a source of increased anxiety to discover that there will be a jury at the inquest. Most professionals will have limited court experience and any knowledge they do have may have come from dramatic and often inaccurate media representations of criminal cases. The role of a jury in an inquest is different from that of a criminal case, and in practice, only about 1 per cent of inquests have a jury (49).

An inquest into a death is held without a jury unless the senior coroner has reason to suspect that it falls into one of the following categories:

1. the deceased died while in custody or otherwise in state detention, and that either:
   (i) the death was violent or unnatural; or
   (ii) the cause of death is unknown.

2. The death resulted from an act or omission of a police officer or a member of a service police force.
3. The death was due to a notifiable accident, poisoning or disease (CJA 2009, section 7).

The coroner also has discretion to summon a jury where these criteria are not met but they are minded that there is 'sufficient reason for doing so'. Guidance is not detailed on this matter, but it can include consideration of the wishes of the family of the deceased and wider public interest in the case.

The decision about whether a jury should be used is normally made early on in proceedings and will often be subject to argument from the interested persons, especially the family. If the coroner does not summon a jury and this decision is proved wrong, through a successful legal challenge, the High Court may order a fresh inquest.

In every jury inquest, the coroner decides matters of law and procedure and the jury decides the facts of the case and reaches a conclusion and findings. The jury is made up of seven to eleven randomly selected members of the public aged 18–65. Unlike in criminal trials, the jury can ask questions of witnesses, but cannot blame someone for the death. The jury will try to reach a unanimous conclusion, but if this does not occur, the coroner has discretion to allow a majority decision if they are satisfied an adequate time has been spent deliberating the relevant issues. If there is any blame, this can only be established by the legal proceedings; in civil or criminal courts, however, in some cases the jury can record facts which make it clear that the death was caused by a specific failure of some sort or by neglect.

Issues Outside the Scope of the Investigation

Any events occurring after the death are outside the scope of the coroner's investigation, such as any investigation into the death by the police. Also outside the scope are questions of policy or resources, although the coroner has a discretion to include them if they may have contributed more than minimally or trivially to the death.

The coroner (or jury) cannot express their view on whether an earlier a legal decision was correctly made. For example, there cannot be criticism of a lawful decision to release a patient from section 3 of the Mental Health Act (section 3 allows for a person to be detained in hospital for treatment if their mental disorder is of a nature and/or degree that requires treatment in hospital), where the patient thereafter left hospital, and subsequently died in the community.

Interested Persons

Gabrielle Pendlebury and Derek Tracy

Key Points

- Giving evidence at the coroner's court does not necessarily make you an 'Interested Person'; this is a formal role or position, designated by the coroner, usually based on professional or personal 'proximity' to the person who has died.
- An organisation (commonly an NHS Trust) as well as an individual can be an Interested Person.
- Individuals less closely professionally connected to the deceased may simply be a witness of fact at court instead of being an Interested Person.
- Some people worry that being an Interested Person means that they are in 'trouble' with the coroner or more likely to face censure. This is not usually the case.
- Being an Interested Person offers some advantages, such as being provided with copies of the inquest documents and being allowed to have legal representation.

It is crucial that a clinician being asked to make a statement in a coroner's court understands their legal status and why they have been asked to participate either as an 'Interested Person' (IP) or as a witness of fact. This is an area that may require legal analysis, but the starting point is always to ask the coroner, your defence organisation or your legal team if you are a witness of fact or an IP. This chapter explains what an IP is and why it is necessary to know your designation.

Who Is an 'Interested Person'?

In simple terms, an IP is someone who has the right to actively participate in the inquest proceedings, whether by virtue of relationship to the deceased, involvement in the circumstances of the death or at the discretion of the coroner. By actively participating, this means having access to the court documents and having legal representation.

There are several statutory grounds under which a person or organisation can be given IP status. These are set out at section 47(2)(a–m) of the CJA 2009. Health and social care professionals are usually recognised as IPs under section 47(2)(f): 'A person who may by any act or omission have caused or contributed to the death of the deceased, or whose employee or agent may have done so.' The coroner also has a 'catch all' discretion in section 47(2)(m) to grant IP status to anyone who is deemed to have 'sufficient interest'. It is advantageous to have IP status, as it allows the witness via their legal representatives to have access to the court documents to be able to ascertain if the professional does require IP status.

If IP status is not triggered by the statutory gateways, there remains the wide 'sufficient interest' provision (section 47(2)(m)). To qualify, there must be:

> ... more than idle curiosity. The mere fact of being a witness will rarely be enough. What must be shown is that the person has a genuine desire to participate more than by the mere giving of relevant evidence in the determination of how, when and where the deceased came by his death (50).

Unlike other legal proceedings, in inquests there are no 'parties', meaning an individual or a group of individuals who can be identified as one for the purposes of the law – for example, the defence and the prosecution in a criminal trial. Instead of parties, IP status is given to those who will need to see the evidence, such as a Trust, an individual professional or a GP.

The Role and Rights of an Interested Person

IPs are identified by the coroner on the basis of the statutory provisions and have the right to legal representation throughout the inquest process. IPs have the right to participate in pre-inquest hearings, where submissions can be made in relation to matters such as scope of the inquest, whether Article 2 is engaged and what evidence is needed. It also gives them the right to disclosure of evidence, to question witnesses at the inquest, and to make submissions on matters of law at the inquest.

Where a person is designated as an IP, their rights include:

1. to be notified of the date, time and place of the inquest hearing (Coroners (Inquests) Rules 2013, Rule 9(2)) and to attend the same;
2. subject to any restrictions on disclosure arising under Rule 15 of the Coroners (Inquests) Rules 2013, to be provided with a document or a copy of that document (Coroners (Inquests) Rules 2013, Rule 13(1));
3. to examine any witness either in person or through their representative (Coroners (Inquests) Rules 2013, Rule 19(1)); and
4. to make submissions to the coroner on matters such as conclusions.

The legal representative of the IP will usually ask questions last, unless there is a jury. Under Rule 19(2) of the Coroners (Inquests) Rules, the coroner must disallow questions that the coroner considers irrelevant.

There can be a fine line between being a witness of fact and an IP and, as a result, a professional may be designated a witness of fact but need to consider whether to seek IP designation. This can be for practical reasons, if all other parties are legally represented, to ensure that the witness is not at a disadvantage ('equality of arms'). Alternatively, it may be because the witness needs to understand their role in the context of the other witnesses, by reading their statements, to be able to participate fully in the inquest.

Requesting 'Interested Person' Status

If a person or organisation believes they may benefit from having IP status, they should discuss the matter with their defence organisation or legal team. The benefits include the ability to make submissions on substantive issues, and to have access to documentation prior to the inquest, to allow the witness to understand where their evidence fits as part of the wider evidence and to also potentially allow an organisation to present evidence to avoid a prevention of future deaths report.

It is preferable to seek IP designation early, to allow your legal representative to be present and active before the Pre-Inquest Review Hearing (PIRH) (Chapter 10). Depending on the outcomes of decisions on scope, for example, the need for continued IP status of an individual may no longer be required. It should also be remembered that there is no general right of appeal to this decision made by the coroner, and that the only action that could be taken after an inquest to challenge whether IP status could or should have been given is a judicial review. Judicial review is a type of court proceeding in which a judge reviews the lawfulness of a decision or action made by a public body (51).

Handling Criticism and Referrals to Professional Regulators

If a Trust or an organisation is criticised at the outset, for example, where the family has expressed concerns, they will usually be identified as an IP. If an individual who works for that body is concerned about criticism specifically being directed at them, and particularly where there is a conflict between their own and other individuals' evidence, they may need to consider whether they should request IP status in their own right. This is a decision that can be made with your defence organisation or legal team. If there is criticism, then you should be informed of the nature of those criticisms. Criticisms may be made not only by the family, but also by other individuals or organisations involved with the deceased, or from the coroner themselves. When constructing your statement, it is important to have an understanding of the reasons for the criticism and the necessary documentation to answer those criticisms, which may be other witness statements, investigation reports, relevant policies and/or the post-mortem examination report.

If an individual clinician is subject to criticism during an inquest about a matter that might concern a regulatory body, it is important to subsequently take advice from your defence organisation about the merits of self-referral to your regulatory body. Coroners have the power to refer professionals to their regulatory bodies, although they are often reluctant to do so. This would follow delivery of their summing up and conclusion containing any criticism. This will not be a shock as you will have been part of the inquest and aware of any issues raised.

Knowing that you have been or will be criticised by the coroner allows the professional to self-refer to the regulator, thus demonstrating a level of insight. Self-referral shows the value that the practitioner attaches to standards and transparency and demonstrates a positive approach to learning. Referral by a coroner to an individual's regulatory body is a rare occurrence, but if it does happen, your defence organisation, legal representative or a solicitor with regulatory expertise can guide the professional through the process and advise on targeted continuing professional development around the issues raised, to demonstrate evidence of remediation to the regulatory body.

Inquest conclusions are not, and cannot be, determinative of civil liability, but the evidence elicited in inquisitorial proceedings can impact on civil claims and IP status can reduce the risk of unanticipated occurrences.

Conflicts of Interest and Separate Representation

It is common for a legal team acting for an organisation, which has been given IP status, to represent that organization, but also to take care of the interests of employees or former employees who are called as witnesses. This gives legal support to the organisation's witnesses from a team with in-depth knowledge of the case and is practically desirable in terms of obtaining the witness evidence required for the inquest, and it avoids unnecessary representation. However, despite the inquisitorial nature of inquests, conflicts do sometimes occur between witnesses, the organisation and other organisational witnesses, and these must be identified and representation separated to meet professional obligations.

Occasionally, conflicts of interest can occur between an organisation and an employee. These can usually be spotted early by considering any internal reviews or independent investigations that may have been undertaken prior to the inquest, where differing accounts of the incident will be evident. Conflicts can arise, for example: when a witness has been disciplined or dismissed by the organisation in relation to their involvement in matters being explored in the inquest; where a witness is critical of an organisation's policy; or where allegations are made by one organisational witness against another.

If serious allegations are being made against a witness by another IP, this should prompt separate representation, even if, strictly speaking, no conflict arises. Inquests can prompt fear and this can on occasion lead to false beliefs relating to the events around the death, but careful review of all documents by the legal representative can usually dispel any false beliefs. Separate and independent representation may be necessary to ensure a fair trial in the rare event that there are subsequent proceedings.

The legal team, whether from your defence organisation, Trust or through independent representation, will be proactively assessing the risk of an actual conflict eventuating, but if you believe that there is a conflict or concern that has been missed, you can discuss this with them. The legal team will have a process in place for identifying and managing potential conflicts and will be able to communicate with the coroner about any representation issues.

Professionals working in primary care or independent practice, as part of a clinic, may be cognisant of potential conflicts that their defence organisation is not aware of; getting these out in the open by being transparent and raising the possibility of potential conflicts early will allow for evaluation and consideration of whether separate representation is required.

8 Deaths Involving Suicide and Unlawful Killing (Homicide Offences)

Gabrielle Pendlebury

Key Points

- The death of a patient by suicide (or homicide) can have a considerable, and lasting, emotional impact on mental health professionals, most commonly manifested as guilt, blame, shock, anger, sadness, anxiety and grief.
- The impact on professionals involved in care is comparable with that of other traumatic life events.
- More should be done to prepare and support mental health professionals for the event that they may lose a patient through suicide (or have a patient commit homicide) (52).

Inquests involving suicide and unlawful killing can be particularly demanding for all involved. This chapter looks at the personal reactions that can occur and will explain the areas that the coroner will be evaluating, namely, there are necessary elements required in each of the homicide offences and the standard of proof required to reach these conclusions.

Deaths involving suicides and homicide offences (unlawful killings) are perhaps the most challenging to professionals and most universally feared. The impact on the professional is not comparable to the devastation experienced by the victim or close relatives of those involved, but there is both a personal and a professional impact. In both instances, there can be a greater sense that something or someone has 'failed' and that an avoidable tragedy has occurred.

Personal Reactions

For many professionals, there will be a complex interplay between their own personality, the circumstances of the death and their past experiences. For some, a propensity to anxiety, depression and feelings of guilt will play a part in their response, making each response personal and potentially very profound. The first reaction is often numbness and a sense of shock; this is normal in any significant loss or bereavement, and, as is also normal where there is significant loss or a bereavement, these are often accompanied by a sense of disbelief and anxiety. At the same time, they may believe they need to act normally to support and lead others, while feeling internally preoccupied and fearful (53).

A sense of shame may separate the professional from their colleagues, sometimes accompanied with concerns that others may regard them as deficient, that they have failed or that their careers are blighted. This can be intermixed with sadness and grief at the loss of a human life and a relationship, and feelings of anger may lead to internal conflict and guilt.

A fear of condemnation by colleagues or, in some instances, the press can engender a sense of public humiliation and may lead to circular ruminations, replaying of details and reviewing of documentation. The inquest and local investigations may mean that such fears eventually do become a reality, and even if this is not the case, such worries about this can be sustained over considerable periods of time.

The Interpretation of Evidence

Professional evidence on the predictors of suicide and violence, the validity and reliability of risk assessments and how such assessments should be interpreted are often useful for the coroner, as there are often misconceptions about the predictive powers of risk assessments and the professionals using them. Suicide and homicidal violence are very difficult to predict and risk assessment tools and scales are not fail-safe. This knowledge is reflected in national guidelines; in the words of the National Institute of Clinical Excellence: 'do not use risk assessment tools and scales to predict future suicide or repetition of self-harm' (54).

Where the deceased falls into what might be considered a 'higher risk' category, such as an in-patient or someone recently discharged from hospital, or if the death was related to opioid prescriptions, evidence will be needed on the prior recognition of this status, and steps taken to mitigate the risks. Information not known by professionals when the person in question was still alive that comes to light in an inquest, whether from family, friends or electronic devices, should be considered by the professional opining on suicidal intent. Unfortunately, secrecy and deception concerning suicidal or homicidal intent are frequently an integral part of the involved person's presentation prior to the event, with many individuals in great distress, but able to mask the extent of it from others. Thus, professionals' opinions or the outcome of an internal investigation presented at the inquest may diverge significantly from the information documented in the medical records at the time of the death, as the investigation may have revealed evidence not available prior to the death.

Suicide

Most individuals who die by suicide in the UK are not in contact with mental health services at the time of their deaths. Between a quarter and a third are in current psychiatric care or had been in the 12 months before their deaths. Prediction of suicide is notoriously difficult, with most patients who die by suicide having been assessed as at low risk at their final service contact, even when this has occurred shortly before death. There are, however, times of particular risk, including the two-week period following discharge from psychiatric inpatient care and also the first few weeks following a hospital presentation for self-harm. While there is evidence that strategies to prevent suicide at the general population level can be effective, and psychiatric services probably prevent numerous suicides (although this is more difficult to demonstrate), identification of patients who are at greater risk than others is extremely difficult. The unpredictability of suicide is one of the factors that makes such deaths of patients under the care of mental health services so challenging for all those involved (55, 52).

For those working in mental health and primary care services, attending a coroner's inquest investigating a death by suicide is not uncommon. It is important to note that the judgement in Maughan (56) held that in inquests, all conclusions (including of suicide and unlawful killing), whether presented in narrative or short form, are to be determined on what is known as the civil standard of proof (proof on balance of probabilities) rather

---

Box 8.1 Changes to the Standard of Proof *R (on the application of Thomas Maughan)* **v.** *HM Senior Coroner for Oxfordshire* (56)

This case raised a discrepancy that had arisen in the way in which the standard of proof was applied to conclusions in respect of unlawful killing and suicide. Short-form conclusions of those causes of death applied the criminal standard of proof, whereas narrative conclusions applied the lower civil standard.

In this case, James Maughan was found hanging in his cell at HMP Bullingdon on 11 July 2016, with a ligature tied around his neck. At the inquest, the coroner directed that the jury could not reach a short-form conclusion of suicide (because the evidence was insufficient to establish suicide to the criminal standard), but invited a narrative conclusion, in which the jury concluded that on the balance of probabilities Mr Maughan had intended fatally to hang himself. His family brought the claim which resulted in this appeal on the basis that that conclusion was not open to the jury because the criminal standard of proof should have been applied to narrative (as well as short-form) conclusions of suicide.

The Supreme Court, by a majority of three to two, disagreed by finding that the civil standard of proof is the correct standard for both short-form and narrative conclusions of suicide, and it extended the same reasoning to the standard of proof that should apply for short-form conclusions of unlawful killing (57).

---

than the criminal standard (proof beyond reasonable doubt). The standard of proof refers to the amount of evidence that is necessary and sufficient to prove an assertion or claim in a trial in court. See Box 8.1.

Unlawful Killing

A conclusion of unlawful killing may only be reached, following an inquest, when the coroner or jury is satisfied on the balance of probabilities that a death was caused by one of the criminal offences detailed in Box 8.2 (58).

These are all relatively rare events for an inquest and healthcare professional to be involved with. For instance, in the year ending March 2023, there were 602 (60) victims of homicide in England and Wales. The homicide rate in the general population has fallen since 2005; however, clinicians working in mental health, particularly forensic services, may be part of a situation where there is a homicide by a patient. The impact of such an event extends beyond the loss of human life, with far-reaching consequences for the perpetrator, their family and friends and those of the victim (61).

Rule 25(4) of the Coroners (Inquests) Rules 2013 requires a coroner to adjourn an inquest and notify the Director of Public Prosecutions if, during the course of the inquest, it appears to the coroner that the death of the deceased is likely to have been due to one of the above offences (that the coroner believes that all elements of the offence may be met on the balance of probabilities) and that a person may be charged in relation to the offence, as happened with Dr Bawa-Garba at the inquest touching on the death of Jack Adcock in 2003 (63):

> (4) A coroner must adjourn an inquest and notify the Director of Public Prosecutions, if during the course of the inquest, it appears to the coroner that the death of the deceased is likely to have been due to a homicide offence and that a person may be charged in relation to the offence (64).

This chapter reviews a complex legal area that may present more questions than answers, but hopefully gives a better understanding of the coroner's analysis in these events.

Box 8.2 The Circumstances in which a Conclusion of Unlawful Killing May Be Reached Following an Inquest

1. **Murder**

   A person is guilty of murder if he/she kills a person unlawfully (namely, not in self-defence or defence of another or accidentally, each of which provides an absolute defence) and at the time intended either to kill the person or cause him/her some really serious bodily harm (murderous intent). A murder is therefore a homicide committed with an intent to kill.

2. **Manslaughter** (including corporate manslaughter)

   There are a number of forms of the offence of manslaughter, the most common form for coroners is gross negligence manslaughter. There is also unlawful act manslaughter, the elements of which (at common law) are:

   i.   a deliberate act which is unlawful (e.g. an assault);

   ii. the act is a dangerous act in that it is, from an objective standpoint, one which a sober, reasonable and responsible person of the perpetrator's age and gender would inevitably realise is an act which is likely to cause the deceased some physical harm, albeit not serious harm; and

   iii. the unlawful, dangerous act causes death (even though death or harm of any kind is not intended).

   Gross negligence manslaughter

   R v. *Rose* (59) summarised the six elements of gross negligence manslaughter as follows:

   1. The defendant owed an existing duty of care to the victim.
   2. The defendant negligently breached that duty of care.
   3. That breach of duty gave rise to an obvious and serious risk of death.
   4. It was also reasonably foreseeable that the breach of that duty gave rise to a serious and obvious risk of death.
   5. The breach of that duty caused the death of the victim.
   6. The circumstances of the breach were truly exceptionally bad and so reprehensible as to justify the conclusion that it amounted to gross negligence and required criminal sanction.

   Each of the six elements of the offence must be established on the balance of probabilities before a coroner or jury may return a conclusion of unlawful killing based upon the offence of gross negligence manslaughter (1).

   Corporate manslaughter is a similar offence committed by an organisation if the way in which its activities are managed or organised causes a person's death and amounts to a gross breach of a relevant duty of care owed to the deceased.

3. **Infanticide**

   Where a woman deliberately or by omission causes the death of her biological child (under the age of 12 months), and the circumstances are such that the offence would otherwise have amounted to murder or manslaughter, she is guilty of the lesser offence of infanticide if at the time of the act or omission the balance of her mind was disturbed by reason of her not having fully recovered from the effect of giving birth to the child, or by reason of the effect of lactation consequent upon the birth.

The Statement (or Report) for the Court

Gabrielle Pendlebury

Key Points

- Write your statement honestly and factually as soon as possible after the death.
- Check your statement carefully before submitting.
- Use a template if you are unsure of the format.

A clinician's first exposure to the coroner is often through a request for a statement. This chapter will explain why such requests are made, their importance, and provide tips and guidance on what makes a good statement (sometimes referred to as a 'report').

Professional Standards

Most healthcare professionals will be touched by an inquest in their professional career and have to produce at least one written report for a coroner. All disciplines will have professional obligations with regard to producing such a statement that focus on being honest.

For doctors, these are set out in the GMC's Good Medical Practice (65), updated in 2024, which states:

> You must be honest and trustworthy when writing reports, and when completing or signing forms, reports and other documents. You must make sure that any documents you write, or sign are not false or misleading.
>
> a. You must take reasonable steps to check the information is correct.
> b. You must not deliberately leave out relevant information.

The duty of confidentiality (66) extends beyond life, but there are exceptions to this rule:

> There are circumstances in which you must disclose relevant information about a patient who has died. For example:
> - when disclosure is required by law
> - to help a coroner, procurator fiscal or other similar officer with an inquest or fatal accident inquiry.

Thus, original medical records and relevant information about the deceased **must** be disclosed to the coroner or the coroner's officer on request.

The Purpose of the Statement

The production of a comprehensive, clear and concise report can have several positive outcomes. It can help the coroner in their understanding of events; give closure to the family by answering questions they have; and provide some catharsis for the clinician, as it is very rare for a clinician not to have doubts about their practice, and if problems or errors are identified, it allows time to address and remediate these before the inquest.

The clinician witness should know why they are being asked to make a statement. The clinician is entitled to ask what questions they should address. For example, it could be to respond to a criticism of care or to state the nature of a condition and its treatment; it could be to establish whether the deceased had an intent to take their life; it could be to explain matters to the family.

General Advice for Preparing a Statement

A well-prepared statement reduces the risk of the coroner asking for clarification. It is also excellent preparation for giving evidence, as the individual, while writing the statement, will be drawn to areas of ambiguity and confusion which may be addressed at this stage rather than remaining unchanged until brought to light at the inquest. It can also reduce the possibility of having to attend the inquest. As per Rule 23 (14) (Chapter 10), the coroner may agree that an undisputed report could be read out at the inquest in your absence.

A statement should be a detailed factual account, and in general it is better to provide too much information rather than too little, though a well-produced summary rather than repetitive reproduction of clinical entries is always welcomed. It should be based on the medical records and your own recollection and your usual practice. In the case of an expert witness (Chapter 12), if you are asked to provide an opinion, you must only comment within your expertise. The writer should also ensure they have had access to the full medical record when preparing their report: the coroner will often require disclosure of the whole medical record.

A statement must be clear and objective, reporting who did what and when. It should also be professional; it is not advisable to use the statement to vent on hospital politics or to criticise others, as this can add to the family's distress. It should also avoid hearsay, second-hand reporting, and speculation – it is the coroner's role to interpret the facts.

General Advice on Writing a Statement

- Write your statement honestly and factually as soon as possible, with reference to the medical records and other relevant documents (incident report forms, theatre lists, ward diary, duty rotas, protocols, etc.).
- Avoid jargon and abbreviations, and remember that, more often than not, the coroner is not medically qualified (Chapter 3). Explain medical terminology, including medication (generic name, dosage and route of administration) and what it is used for. The coroner and the family will appreciate this and it will reduce the need for further explanations. Someone with no medical knowledge should be able to read and understand your statement.
- The statement should stand on its own. Do not assume that all readers will have access to the medical records or knowledge of the case.

- It may be useful to use a template (see example below).
- Divide your statement up into clear paragraphs. Numbering paragraphs may make it easier to refer to sections of your report in case you are asked to give evidence. This can be particularly helpful in what can feel a very stressful environment as you are on the stand giving testimony in the coroner's court, and save anxious page-turning back and forth trying to find the correct part of a statement. There is no clear stylistic 'rule' as to whether you should use bullet points or more 'free flowing' narrative text.
- Write in the first-person singular – 'I did this . . .'
- Type your statement on headed paper using full, grammatically correct sentences. Individuals' confidence about their written English, especially the more formal type required by a court, can be daunting for some, especially if it is not their first language. While it can be helpful to have a trusted colleague or friend check and comment on some aspects, remember that the rules of confidentiality still apply, and any shared information must be suitably anonymised. A Trust legal team or your indemnifier/medical defence organisation may also be able to assist, and some organisations run courses on report writing, highlighting good and bad examples.
- Do not exceed your level of competence by attempting to speak for other disciplines.
- Do not deliberately conceal or intentionally minimise anything, as this may make your other evidence less credible and could become a probity issue.
- Do not rush it.
- Check your statement for errors: even minor grammatical errors can be viewed negatively through the lens of grief, so asking someone else to proofread your final statement and identify any errors can avoid misperceptions (65).
- Look at the overall impact: does the narrative have good sequencing and coherence so that the reader can visualise how events occurred?
- Sign and date your statement before sending it to the coroner. This should be done with the knowledge and agreement of the Trust or organisation, usually the Chief Medical Officer/Medical Director or Chief Nurse/Director of Nursing, or delegated by them to a legal team or service.
- Keep a copy and a note of how, when and to whom you submitted it. Email and postal systems can fail and it may be worth asking for confirmation of receipt.

What the report should include:

- Your full name and your qualifications, number of years working, relevant clinical experience and grades, and background.
- Describe your role at the time you saw the patient (e.g. social worker, GP registrar, nurse, consultant). Be specific about where and in what capacity you saw the patient (e.g. NHS or private, on the ward or in an out-patient clinic, as the patient's usual treating clinician or as an on-call or emergency first review).
- Relevant local factors – for example, the hospital being on two sites or being on call from home may affect the time taken to get to a review or incident.
- Patient details.
- Your observations and understanding via a detailed chronological account of your interaction with the deceased. This may include history that you were given, an examination or investigation that took place and their findings (if another was present, include their name and status, for example, spouse, social worker, etc.). Also

include any negative findings, as these can help to demonstrate that that condition was considered. Include your differential diagnosis, management plan/follow-up arrangements and any safety netting advice that was given, if appropriate.

- It can be very helpful to describe 'negative findings' in terms of clinical decisions **not** made and **why** – for example, why you decided against admitting an individual to hospital and what the safety plan was.
- Consider what is **not** included in the medical notes. Just as negative findings (e.g. pulse was regular, ECG was normal) are often important in clinical reports, it may also be important to note events that were not formally recorded. For example, the lack of entries to show parents sought medical advice for injuries may raise a safeguarding concern, if evidence of healed fractures is later found during a post-mortem.
- Outline any hospital referrals, identifying the name of the relevant practitioner or consultant and any other clinicians involved in the care of the deceased.
- Specify what the different details of your account are based on. This could be your memory, the contemporaneous notes you or others wrote, or your usual or normal practice.

Appendix 1 contains an example template for a statement for the coroner.

Supplementary Statements

On occasion, a supplementary statement may be required to deal with issues that come to light after you wrote your original statement. Before doing this, make sure that you review your statement, the medical records and any new documentation.

Pre-Inquest Review Hearing and Rule 23

10

Gabrielle Pendlebury

Key Points

- The PIRH assists in the efficient management of the inquest.
- The coroner may be guided by the legal representatives as to who would be an appropriate witness.
- Rule 23 allows for witness statements to be submitted in writing, as opposed to orally at the inquest.

The Purpose of a Pre-Inquest Review Hearing

The coroner may hold a pre-inquest review hearing (PIR or PIRH) at any time or this may be held after the interested persons (IPs) submit their statements. The purpose is to decide on the scope of the investigation, ask for disclosure of information, identify witnesses and plan the inquest date and duration. This chapter will explain this process.

A PIRH is an administrative hearing that is typically held where an inquest is complex or involves a number of IPs, but they are becoming increasingly common, even in simpler inquests. All IPs or their representatives will usually be present. The purpose of the PIRH is to assist in the management of the inquest itself, which is particularly useful in complex cases. It is organised to ensure that the inquest runs smoothly through advance consideration of the issues and in a transparent and open manner. Thus, it will often be the case that a professional will **not** be called to a PIRH. Being called, or not called, to a PIRH does not signify the severity or seriousness of the issues, or infer any judgement on the clinician's role in events. It is merely to assist the coroner plan the inquest when this is deemed helpful. Nevertheless, a PIRH is usually welcomed by IPs, as it allows their legal teams to obtain an early understanding of the evidence and engagement with witnesses to ensure the inquest is accurate, fair and appropriately focused.

Part of the process is to define who will give evidence and how. For example, either before the inquest or at the PIRH, if a professional is being called to give live evidence, but their defence organisation or legal representative feels that the statement could be read, an application can be made in writing to have the statement read under Rule 23 of the Coroners (Inquests) Rules 2013 (SI 2013 No. 1616) (14).

Preparing for a Pre-Inquest Review Hearing

The hearing is usually the first opportunity that IPs have to make submissions on scope, issues, evidence, disclosure, witnesses and the overall conduct of the inquest. This means that lots of preparation is undertaken by the legal parties to allow for effective use of this hearing. For the clinician, this may mean sessions with their legal team or defence organisation to understand exactly what they did in relation to the deceased and their rationale for those decisions.

Coroners usually provide a written agenda in advance of all PIRHs to give IPs notice of the topics under discussion and time for preparation (67). The agenda will cover matters such as IP status, issues, scope, Article 2, juries, disclosure, witnesses, timetabling and listing.

If no agenda is available, the IP's legal representative will request one to allow for the necessary preparation. If you work for an NHS Trust, this will likely be arranged by a legal team or department within the organisation without you even being aware; in other circumstances, you may need to liaise with your defence organisation. The coroner may provide their provisional views as part of the agenda to allow IPs to identify areas of agreement and opposition, and in more complex inquests or in contentious matters, IPs may be asked to provide written submissions in advance.

Witnesses

Coroners have a wide discretion to decide which witnesses to call and the PIRH is an opportunity to make suggestions about who should be called. The coroner can be guided as to who would be an appropriate witness. The coroner will not call everyone who might give relevant evidence, but will call sufficient witnesses to undertake a full inquiry. A provisional witness list is usually circulated and IPs can then make comment.

Relevant witnesses of fact can often be overlooked in complex medical situations, where the coroner may not be fully aware of the systems. If prevention of future deaths evidence will be needed, this gives IPs the ability to identify who would be best placed to provide that.

The Presence of Witnesses (Rule 23)

Under the Coroners (Inquests) Rules 2013 (14), it is not always necessary for a witness or IP to attend in person. Coroners are acutely aware of the pressures faced by healthcare workers and the potential need for clinical cover. It may therefore be appropriate for a witness's or IP's legal representative to consider whether Rule 23 can be employed and make a written request to the coroner.

This rule allows for evidence (witness statements) to be admitted in writing as opposed to orally at the inquest. However, professionals should note that the bar for this is set relatively high, and mere work inconvenience will not be considered a valid excuse. Ordinarily, as sufficient time will have been provided to IPs, issues such as clinical and on-call cover will be expected to have been obtained. Even pre-booked annual leave may be challenged by the coroner. This may be acceptable if the coroner is satisfied that:

1. it is not possible for the maker of the written evidence to give evidence at the inquest hearing at all, or within a reasonable time;

2. there is a good and sufficient reason why the maker of the written evidence should not attend the inquest hearing;
3. there is a good and sufficient reason to believe that the maker of the written evidence will not attend the inquest hearing; or
4. the written evidence (including evidence in admission form) is unlikely to be disputed.

Is Article 2 Engaged?

As previously explained, the fundamental purpose of any inquest is to answer the four statutory questions and when it is an Article 2 inquest (see Chapter 6), the scope of investigating the 'how' question can be considerably wider than in a traditional hearing.

A coroner decides how wide this scope should be. This decision is based on their view as to what is necessary, desirable and proportionate for this investigation to discharge its statutory function (68). This gives them considerable discretion in determining scope, but that discretion is not absolute. Where Article 2 is engaged, the coroner has a discretion (but not a duty) to investigate issues which may have contributed towards the death, but not those which cannot even arguably be said to have contributed (69).

In general terms, the threshold for Article 2 engagement is low (70) and, in many cases, it will be obvious that it is engaged (e.g. a death while in police custody or a self-inflicted death while under a section of the Mental Health Act, while being detained in hospital).

Since medical cases and deaths in hospital can be highly complex, they may result in a great deal of legal argument during the PIRH. This may impact all IPs involved in an inquest, as when Article 2 is engaged, it is engaged for everyone. If it is engaged, the coroner will then consider if a jury is required. Where it is unclear if a jury is required, the coroner decides based on whether they suspect the cause of death would meet the criteria. The coroner may exercise their discretion by taking into account all relevant matters, including: the wishes of the family (which are relevant, but not determinative); submissions on behalf of other IPs; whether the facts resemble the types of situation where a jury is mandated; the circumstances of the death; any uncertainties in the medical evidence; the need for a reasoned judgement; and factors such as whether the inquest will be very document-heavy or relate to historical matters (71).

Article 2 being engaged is not determinative of the question of whether a jury is required. It is usual for the coroner to determine the scope of an inquest before considering whether to summon a jury (72). It should be noted that while the threshold for engaging Article 2 is low, that for determining an actual breach of an individual's rights under this – namely, serious and immediate risk to life – is typically quite high.

The Professional as a Witness

Gabrielle Pendlebury

Key Points

- The coroner decides which witnesses to call to best assist proceedings.
- Do not provide opinions on areas beyond your expertise.
- Make sure you know whether you are expected to attend the coroner's court or if the inquest is being held remotely.

Attending an inquest as a witness can provoke anxiety. Professionals called as witnesses of fact may have heard stories about colleagues who have received prolonged questioning from barristers representing families in emotionally charged hearings. It may feel very uncomfortable to have to justify decisions, which are often taken in difficult and dynamic scenarios with multiple pressures, including resource issues and without the full picture that emerges with hindsight. Although not all inquests run smoothly for the clinician, most witnesses experience some catharsis following an inquest as they finally feel able to put the inquest behind them, with the knowledge that they have explained what happened clearly and professionally, assisting both the coroner and the relatives of the deceased to better understand what has occurred.

Professionals are routinely called to supply factual information obtained in their professional role in a particular case. The coroner decides what witnesses to call to give evidence, based on their perceptions of how this will best assist proceedings. As similarly noted in Chapter 10 on pre-inquest hearings, being called to give oral testimony does not infer likely blame or responsibility on the professional, but merely shows that the coroner wishes to better understand that individual's perspectives through questioning. Nevertheless, professionals called to participate as an interested person should be aware that this would indicate that the coroner believes them to be more *centrally* involved in the circumstances leading to the death and that they may be subject to criticism or require equal legal representation in the interests of fairness, if other witnesses are legally represented. A failure by a coroner to call relevant witnesses may be a ground to quash the inquest and order a fresh inquest to be heard (73). Where there have been a series of failings, the High Court has held that it is necessary to call witnesses who have direct knowledge and responsibility in relation to the treatment of the patient (74). Clinicians can discuss with their legal advisers which witnesses are most appropriate to be suggested to the coroner, although ultimately the decision is that of the coroner.

Clinicians frequently play a pivotal role in proceedings. Whether they are an interested person (Chapter 7) or not, professionals may be called either as witnesses of fact (e.g. a treating clinician) or as expert witnesses (e.g. a professional retained in that capacity as an expert by the coroner), or both (e.g. a forensic pathologist). Their written statement will form the basis of their oral evidence and they may be asked relevant questions to clarify certain aspects. A professional who is a witness (whether a witness of fact or an expert witness) is entitled to be remunerated (75) and they are paid according to scales set by the Secretary of State. However, if receiving your usual salary during days of attendance at court, it would be prudent to discuss this with your employer, as a payment from both could be mistakenly interpreted as a probity issue. In our experience, professionals who attend as a witness of fact invariably continue to be paid by their employer while attending the coroner's inquest and do not claim this remuneration.

Advice to the Professional Who Is a Witness

It is important to stick to the facts, and not to stray into providing opinion on areas beyond your expertise. You are being asked to provide factual information obtained in your professional role in a particular case.

You must be honest and trustworthy when giving evidence; this means making sure any evidence you give or documents you write, or sign, are not false or misleading and that you recognise and work within the limits of your competence. What is expected of professionals depends on their specific workplace and role, but some general expectations in this context are summarised in Box 11.1.

It is usual to be put on notice that your attendance is required. This is to allow to the professional to make practical arrangements such as getting cover for their work during their absence. At this stage, you can alert the coroner's officer to any times that may be difficult for you as there may be some leeway to the timings of witnesses. As noted in Chapter 10, the bar is set higher than many clinicians realise, and, for example, merely having a pre-booked clinic or being on-call on a given date is quite unlikely to serve as an adequate reason not to attend: the expectation is that such obligations can be rescheduled. It may be possible to arrange for remote attendance via online technology, but this will need clarifying and agreement with the coroner's office.

In some cases, you will receive a letter, but at other times a witness summons. In either case, you must attend at the specified time and for the set duration. Failure to comply with a witness summons or refusal to answer questions could result in you

---

Box 11.1 Relevant paragraphs from *Good Medical Practice* (updated in 2024) (65)

- You must be familiar with guidelines and developments that affect your work.
- You must keep up to date with, and follow, the law, our guidance and other regulations relevant to your work.
- You must recognise and work within the limits of your competence.
- You must be honest and trustworthy when giving evidence to courts or tribunals.
- You must make sure that any evidence you give or documents you write or sign are not false or misleading.
- You must take reasonable steps to check the information.
- You must not deliberately leave out relevant information.
- You must cooperate with formal inquiries and complaints procedures and must offer all relevant information while following the guidance in *Confidentiality*.
- You must make clear the limits of your competence and knowledge when giving evidence or acting as a witness.

Box 11.2 To prepare for an inquest

- Read through your statement.
- Review the medical records.
- Be clear who has called you to attend.
- Find out where the court is and how long it will take you to get there.
- Find out how long you will be needed for.
- Make sure the medical records will be available at the court.
- Make sure you have adequate cover arrangements in place.

Box 11.3 To prepare for a remote hearing online

- Check the digital platform that the court will be using and ensure that you have this installed on your device in advance, or that you will be able to connect via a link without installation being necessary.
- Ask for a test run from the court to ensure that the remote link works with your equipment.
- Check you have all the relevant documents (disclosure bundle, a copy of your statement, medical records, etc.).
- If you are planning to take the oath on a religious text or affirm, let the court know in advance, as you will then be sent a set paragraph to read out before you give your evidence.
- It is essential to ensure that you will be providing evidence and listening to proceedings in a private, undisturbed space. Coroners are likely to look very unfavourably upon witnesses who are interrupted by others, or where others are visible or audible in the background.

being found in contempt of court (76), which is a criminal offence (Chapter 3). If you have legitimate reasons for not being able to attend, discuss this early with your legal adviser. See Boxes 11.2 and 11.3 for a summary of how to prepare for an inquest and a remote hearing online.

Self-Incrimination

An area that witnesses can be concerned about is the possibility of self-incrimination. In an inquest, a witness is not obliged to answer any question tending to incriminate him or her in a criminal matter, and where the coroner believes that a witness has been asked such a question, the coroner must inform the witness that he or she may refuse to answer it (14). A hypothetical example may be a direct question asking if a medication error that you made led to the death of a patient. In a situation such as this, there may be many factors and the medication error may be only one, and you would be able to answer that you are unable to answer that question.

In relation to answering questions that would expose the witness to a professional disciplinary charge (e.g. NMC or General Medical Council Fitness to Practice Panel), the privilege is not engaged, as the function of the proceedings is to protect the public rather than to help or hinder any processes relating to how professions regulate themselves. A hypothetical question may be: Did you alter the medical records after the death of the patient? In this instance, no criminal charge would arise from this, but a disciplinary one may, so you would not be able to decline to answer that question.

12

Expert Witnesses in the Coroner's Court

Keith Rix

Key Points
- Experts have an overriding duty to help the court with matters within their expertise, to assist with impartial evidence.
- The coroner decides which expert witnesses to call.
- Research and preparation are essential, do not neglect to consider opposing opinions.

Coroners have a wide discretion in the calling of witnesses, including expert witnesses. This chapter looks briefly at the role of experts in the coroner's court, admissibility of expert evidence and some factors that experts consider when writing a report.

Acting as an expert witness requires careful thought, training and preparation and there are numerous texts (77) that can support you on this journey, but hopefully this brief overview will be beneficial to all readers and will set prospective experts off on the right path. It is worth emphasising that most professionals acting as witnesses in coronial proceedings are **not** expert witnesses, but are there as a witness of fact or an interested person (IP). An expert witness will not have been directly involved in the case before the coroner, but will have been instructed to attend and provide evidence given their specific expertise in at least one of the areas being reviewed by the coroner.

The Expert Witness in the Coroner's Court

Experts have an overriding duty to help the court with matters within their expertise, by assisting with independent and impartial evidence. This overrides any obligation to the person that has instructed them. In the coroner's court, the duty of the professional matches that of the coroner: to assist or aid fully, fairly and fearlessly (11). Fully means no short cuts. Fairly means applying independence and objectivity. Fearlessly means not being afraid to criticise fellow professionals or to defend the practice of fellow professionals who have been criticised by advocates for IPs.

Admissibility of Expert Evidence

Coroners have a wide discretion in the calling of witnesses. The coroner decides what evidence to admit as to the death (78), what evidence is relevant (79) and what relevant evidence is needed (80). This discretion applies to the calling of expert witnesses (81). Even in the case of an Article 2 inquest (Chapter 6), there is no principle that independent expert evidence is always required. It was contended in *Chambers* v. *HM Coroner for Preston and West Lancashire* (82), a case of a prison suicide, that independent psychiatric evidence should be called, but the Divisional Court rejected this, stating that each case must be decided on its own facts. If an IP wishes to call expert evidence, it can make a submission to the coroner 'so that the coroner may be able to decide whether or not it is appropriate' (83).

In a personal injury action, if an expert prepares a report that is not supportive of their instructing party's case and the report is subject to legal privilege, then it only exceptionally has to be disclosed. However, in the coroner's court, if an expert is instructed by an interested party to prepare a report and that report does not support criticisms that the interested party may have of one or more of the other interested parties, the report may still be disclosed and the expert potentially called to give oral testimony. It is similar in a criminal case in which a report commissioned by the prosecution is disclosable, whether or not it supports the prosecution's case; this disclosure can result in the prosecution's expert being called to give evidence by the defence.

Investigating the Case

The first stage in the investigation of a coronial case by an expert witness is the construction of a time-line or chronology. Of the four questions, it is the 'how' question about which the court is most likely to require expert evidence. This goes beyond the simple question of the medical cause. 'How' can be widely interpreted, but, in this context, it means 'by what means' rather than in what broad circumstances (84). So, the inquiry focuses on matters directly causative of death and is confined to these matters alone.

In *R* v. *HM Coroner for Inner London West District, ex parte Dallaglio* (85), it was noted that:

> the Court ... did not however rule that the investigation into the means by which the deceased came by his death should be limited to the last link in the chain of causation ... It is for the coroner conducting an inquest to decide, on the facts of a given case at what point the chain of causation becomes too remote to form a proper part of his investigation.

Indeed, to limit it to the last link in the chain of causation would defeat the purpose of holding inquests at all. Box 12.1 illustrates how the coroner's decision on the scope of an inquest can be legally challenged.

Preparing the Expert Report

The purpose of this section is to highlight some points and indicate some differences between a 'generic' and an expert report.

The Writer

The first section about 'The Writer' of the report should, as always, summarise the expert's relevant knowledge and experience. It is imperative to remain within your expertise; if questions are asked about areas outside of your expertise, you may advise the instruction of an expert or experts in those fields and to whose expertise you make it clear that you will defer.

> **Box 12.1** The scope of an inquest is as wide as the coroner deems necessary, but can be challenged
>
> Pavlos Takoushis (83), who had a long history of schizophrenia, and was an inpatient, failed to return from ground leave. Later that day, he was seen preparing to jump from a bridge into the River Thames. Taken to a nearby hospital, triage established that he was at high risk of self-harm and needed attention within 10 minutes, as per the categorisation of the patient and the hospital policy. This did not happen. He left the hospital and jumped to his death in the River Thames. The Court of Appeal held that there had not been a proper investigation as to whether a systemic failure had allowed the circumstances of his death to occur. The coroner had failed to 'investigate how the system was to work [after initial triage] and did not consider, for example, what was to be done and in particular what safeguards were in place if for some reason the patient could not be seen in the target time'.
>
> Judgement is needed as to the extent of the investigation.

Conflicts of Interest

Inquiry should have been made at the outset as to whether or not the proposed expert knows any of the staff involved in, or has or had any connection with anybody responsible for, the care of the deceased. If there is such knowledge or involvement and which the coroner or the instructing party has agreed is not sufficient to constitute a conflict of interest, it must nevertheless be mentioned.

The Chronology

The chronology should cover four domains: (1) date (and time); (2) the nature of the episode – for example, general practitioner consultation, or the name of the person – for example, Florence Nightingale, community mental health nurse; (3) the facts, using quotation marks if quoting *verbatim* from a document; and (4) the page or document reference, preferably using a referencing system already adopted, but, if not, one created by the expert so that they, at least, will be able easily to locate the source of the information. Use regular font for contemporaneous information and use *italic* type for non-contemporaneous information such as that contained in witness statements.

Creating the Narrative

The main part of the body of any expert report is the section 'Facts or Assumed Facts' or the 'Factual Analysis'. This is the section in which to create the factual narrative which will be used as the springboard for the 'Opinion' or the answers to the questions that have been put by the coroner or the instructing interested party. In many expert reports, the facts are assembled under various headings; in an independent expert report for the coroner's court, it is usually advisable to set out the history as far as possible chronologically so that the story of the deceased's life and death gradually unfolds. Of course, this process is so much easier if the chronology has been created with sufficient thoroughness and accuracy. Headings and sub-headings can be used to break up this section.

There are two conventions for the explanation or definition of medical and technical terms. One is to embolden the word or words when first used and to create an appendix of medical and technical terms. The other is to create a series of footnotes on the pages of the report on which the word or term is first mentioned. Some experts do both. In a report for a coroner, for reasons explained below, it is better to use footnotes.

Answering the Questions

The 'Opinion' section is the place to answer the questions, or offer an opinion on the issues, in the case. Usually, they will have been set out with some particularity, in which case each question or issue becomes a sub-heading. Sometimes, there are overlapping questions or issues, in which case the expert can simplify them, but, however this section is structured, the expert must ensure that they deal with all of the questions or issues unless any fall outside their expertise or there is insufficient information.

The Opinion should be followed by a 'Summary of the Conclusions' or what is sometimes called an 'Executive Summary'.

The Inquest: Preparing for Court

Preparation for going to court is in some ways more demanding than in civil and criminal cases, where you are likely to have had a conference with the team and at which counsel will have tested your evidence clarifying its strengths and weaknesses. Not so in the coroner's court; there is the risk that you only become aware of the weaknesses when questioned by one or more of the IPs.

Giving Evidence

Before you go into the witness box, make sure that you know how the court is referring to the deceased. Usually, it will be by the deceased's forename, although in your report you will probably have referred to 'the Deceased'. You will be called to the witness box and someone should already have ascertained whether you will take the oath on a religious text or affirm. The oath and affirmation are not the same as the ones most often used in criminal and other proceedings. Look at the coroner when you take the oath or make your affirmation.

You will be taken through your evidence either by the coroner or by counsel acting for the coroner. If the coroner is sitting without a jury, make sure that you face the coroner and direct your answers to him or her. If there is a jury, make sure that they can hear you.

As soon as you have taken the oath or affirmed and, usually, been invited to sit, express your condolences to the deceased's family and, if you have identified them in court, look towards them when you do so.

You are likely to be asked first about your qualifications, training and experience. Coroners and their counsel vary in how they elicit expert evidence. Exceptionally, you may be asked to read out the whole of the body of your report, or the Opinion or the Summary of Conclusions in its entirety. More often, you will be asked to read out particular paragraphs from these. When asked a question about a conclusion in the Summary of Conclusions, be able to turn back to the corresponding paragraph in the Opinion for context or reasoning. And remember when you are reading from the report to substitute the deceased's name for 'the Deceased'.

After the coroner or their counsel has elicited your evidence, you are likely to be asked questions by counsel for the interested parties. They may include one or more

NHS trusts, other relevant organisations and the deceased's family. Counsel for the family usually goes last. If the family has been unable to obtain legal representation, you may be asked questions by one or more family members. If you have identified any potential failings, although the proceedings are inquisitorial, you can expect searching questions from one or more parties, much like a cross-examination in adversarial proceedings. However, even though '[a]ny overtly adversarial approach to inquest advocacy is now likely to be firmly criticised and even the subject of referral to professional bodies', it is permissible to challenge you or put it to you in plain terms that you are wrong (86). After questions from the IPs, if there is a jury, there may be questions from the jury. Sometimes, these give rise to further questions from the IPs.

Afterwards

Some coroners will send you a copy of their, or the jury's, conclusions and, if the coroner makes one, a Prevention of Future Death report (Chapter 16). If you do not receive a copy of the conclusions, you are advised to ask for one and for a copy of any PFD. The PFD may include feedback on your evidence which you can include in the material submitted for your annual appraisal.

Getting Paid

The Coroners Allowances, Fees and Expenses Regulations 2013 (87) set out 'Expert witness fee for preparatory work' and 'Expert witness fee for attending an inquest':

Expert witness fee for preparatory work

A coroner may pay an expert witness who has carried out preparatory work directly related to the giving of evidence at an inquest a fee that the coroner considers reasonable having regard to the nature and complexity of the preparatory work carried out.

Expert witness fee for attending an inquest

(1) A coroner may pay an expert witness a fee that the coroner considers reasonable for attending and giving expert evidence at an inquest.

(2) When considering a fee which is reasonable ... the coroner shall have regard to the nature and complexity of the evidence provided by the expert witness.

Such fees should be negotiated and agreed upon instruction. Likewise, where the expert is instructed, it is for the expert to negotiate and agree their fees and expenses with the instructing party. It is important to bear in mind that the families of the deceased may not be entitled to any legal aid funding, in which case consideration needs to be given to charging an 'uneconomic' fee, acting *pro bono* or charging a fee and then making a charitable donation to the charity which is funding the family.

But, as in any case in which a doctor assists a court or tribunal with expert assistance, more important than financial reward is the rewarding knowledge that you have assisted in the administration of justice.

Chapter 13

On the Day
Giving Evidence

Mark Tarn and Gabrielle Pendlebury

Key Points
- Preparation is key. Practically plan your journey to the inquest so you are not late.
- Remain professional at all times.
- Relatives can be distressed and this can be evident in their questioning; remain calm, the coroner will support you if needed.

The day of the inquest has finally arrived. This chapter gives an understanding of the court setting and proceedings, and practical tips on how to prepare for the day and give evidence effectively.

The Court Setting

In most courts, the coroner sits at the head of the courtroom, with the witness box usually to one side. The advocates' bench faces the front of the coroner and behind that is general seating. Inquests are held in an open (public) forum, and some will generate media attention, so reporters may be present. Some recent inquests have had the very contemporary phenomenon of members of the public 'tweeting' and making other forms of live social media posting on events. This can feel unsettling for clinicians, especially if they are named in these, but it is lawful if the coroner has given permission (88).

Live, text-based communications by journalists or legal commentators for the sole purpose of fair and accurate reporting are permitted at all hearings, in accordance with the Lord Chief Justice's guidelines for court proceedings: Practice Guidance, 2011 (89). Other members of the public who wish to make records in this way must apply to the coroner for permission. No application need be made by journalists or legal commentators. Except for these purposes, mobile phones must be switched off.

The current law requires that the coroner and the jury must attend court in person. The Chief Coroner has indicated that new rules will be introduced to allow for remote attendance by coroners and juries, but this is likely to only apply in exceptional circumstances. Interested persons (IPs) may submit a recommendation of who should be in court and witnesses may request permission to participate remotely (14).

Following the COVID-19 pandemic, it has become much more common for inquests to be held partly remotely, with the coroner in court and the witnesses and IPs remote. For the press and public, there may also sometimes be a hybrid arrangement where they may be admitted via an audio line.

However, it should be noted that remote attendance at hearings by witnesses (and observers) will not be allowed purely for the convenience of the participant. *The Chief Coroner considers it is often beneficial for participants to attend hearings in person and that remote attendance should not normally be permitted purely because a participant would prefer it.* It is, however, an option available if it will improve the quality of the evidence or expedite the hearing.

The interests of justice are very broad and each coroner will be under different pressures. The coroner must consider whether remote attendance would impede the questioning of the witness (14). Resources may also be a factor, as well as the circumstances of the individual case in holding an effective hearing. Coroners will balance the interests of justice and the interests of all those attending the proceedings.

Court Proceedings

On the day, the coroner, to be addressed as 'Sir' or 'Madam', will outline the purpose of the inquest. The coroner will then read out the order of events and how the day will proceed in terms of who and when each witness will take the stand. This gives participants an indication of where they are 'placed' (if they are not aware of this already).

At some point, the family may be invited to give a pen portrait summarising their view of the deceased person's life (Box 13.1).

For witnesses who are attending in person, when it is their turn, they will be invited into court and shown into the witness box.

If a jury hearing with remote participants takes place, the jury must be visible to all remote participants. Witnesses will be warned that recording or broadcasting proceedings is prohibited. This is not the same as the press or members of the public reporting on what is happening via other forms of media with permission from the coroner. Below is an example of an oral warning regarding recording and broadcasting to participants attending via video link:

> I give permission for the use of live video to enable participants to access these proceedings. It is a contempt of court to record, play, or publish a recording or transcript of the proceedings, or to dispose of a recording or transcript with a view to its publication. That means that if you record or broadcast any part of these proceedings, you will be committing a criminal offence. (91)

Box 13.1   The Pen Portrait

A number of recent inquests of national importance have used pen portraits to humanise the process and give dignity to the bereaved. It can also help the coroner to determine one of the four statutory questions, namely, 'who' the deceased was.

The coroner will generally ask the family to tell the court something about their loved one, to gain an impression of them in life – what he or she did, their interests and hobbies, and details of their wider circle of family and friends. Some families will want to do this. As part of forming this pen portrait, families may also be asked if they have any family photographs that the coroner can see (90).

The coroner will make it clear to the jury (if one is present) that the pen portrait is a reflection of the person in life rather than in death and is not a matter of evidence to be taken into account when deciding on the conclusion. In exceptional circumstances, it may not be appropriate to allow the use of pen portraits.

Although it is illegal to take your own recording of proceedings (Criminal Justice Act 1925, section 4192(a)), all hearings are audio recorded and IPs have the right to have a copy of the court recording and can request this.

The process of questioning a witness follows a set order. First, the witness will be asked to swear a religious oath or affirmation, depending on their preference. The witness will then be questioned (examined) by the coroner. This will be thorough and detailed as the coroner needs to fully understand what happened. Next, other parties will then have the opportunity to question the witness. This includes the family, who are at the heart of the inquest process. Finally, the legal representative of the witness (if there is one) will ask questions to correct or clarify anything that is not clear. It is important to confirm in advance if you will have legal representation on the day, or if you will be attending alone. Chapter 15 gives advice, from a legal advocate's perspective and experience, about managing questioning in court from a barrister or advocate.

The witness is usually released from their oath by the coroner and free to leave (or to stay and watch) after their evidence is complete. Occasionally, the witness may remain under oath during a break or overnight; if this is the case, they cannot discuss your evidence with anyone else during this time. On rare occasions, a later witness may contradict their evidence on the same issue; if this happens, they might be re-called.

At the end of the inquest, the conclusion will be read out, either short-form or, more often, when state bodies are involved, a 'narrative verdict' that explains the story. The word 'verdict' was previously used, but this was changed to 'conclusion' in 2009, as it was associated with criminal or civil trials. The whole process of hearing the evidence in the course of the inquest and not just the conclusion is beneficial for families to aid closure.

Advice on Preparing for the Day

Ideally, you will have had a look at the court before the day of the inquest. If this is your first inquest and you have not attended one before, it can be useful to go and see another inquest that is heard before the one you are to attend. Inquests are open to the public, although it is a courtesy to inquire with the court in advance about attendance, as there can be issues that might make this less convenient or suitable. Further, many courts now offer advance visits to witnesses to be shown around and orientated to the specific court.

This can often allay any fears you may have and make the day of the inquest less daunting and disorientating. A visit may also give you an opportunity to meet the coroner's officer who is dealing with the case. If this is not possible, your legal representative can orientate you, as they will know the set up and how that court works.

There is no formal dress code, but dress professionally or in uniform out of respect for the family of the deceased person. A good 'rule of thumb' is to *wear* what you would consider appropriate *attire* for a job interview.

When on the witness stand, it is helpful to stand with your feet pointed towards the coroner as that is a useful physical reminder that all your answers need to be directed to the coroner (and jury if there is one).

Medical records and documents should be available to you if you need to refer to them; it is your responsibility to check that they are available. Witnesses have noted that on occasion they have not been available, so having a separate set of the relevant notes/documents available can be very useful. If you need to refer to them about a specific detail, take your time to ensure your evidence is factually accurate.

Advice for Attending Remotely

If attending remotely, via virtual means such as Teams or Zoom, be as ready as you would be for court.

- Test your connection beforehand.
- Prepare the room (wherever you are giving evidence is an extension of the court room, so ensure no patient-identifiable information is behind you).
- Ensure your phone is switched off.
- Do not communicate with others while giving evidence, such as via the chat function.
- Make sure you will not be interrupted.
- For more information on giving evidence at a remote hearing, see Box 13.2.

General Advice on Giving Evidence

- The coroner will take you through who you are and your role by asking you to introduce yourself. You should include in your introduction your role, title, years of experience, any specialist background and how you came to know the deceased.
- The coroner may ask you to read your statement, or you may be asked a series of questions depending on how the coroner wants to elicit evidence.
- It is appropriate to commence by expressing your condolences on the death of the deceased.
- You should be open and honest and thorough in response. If asked awkward or difficult questions, try not to overthink, listen carefully and answer the question honestly and straightforwardly.
- Remember that you are not there to defend the institution, an individual or yourself. The primary role of the witness is to explain to the court and the family of the deceased what happened from your perspective. That is what you did and saw, and what happened. You have been called by the coroner as a witness after they have carefully considered who has the best grasp of the facts they are interested in and who can offer the 'most' help in understanding the circumstances surrounding this person's death. The key to giving evidence in an inquest is that it should be about explaining. Understanding the factors that led to a key decision are usually more important in an inquest than the actual decision.

Box 13.2 Giving Evidence at a Remote Hearing

- You must be alone when you give your evidence, unless you have permission from the court for someone to be present.
- Ensure that you are ready at least 15 minutes before the start time.
- Ensure your phone is switched off.
- Do not record the hearing.
- If the connection fails during the course of your evidence, don't panic – just try to reconnect. If this isn't possible, call the court and explain the position.
- Once your evidence is completed, check with the coroner or judge that they are content for you to leave the hearing.
- If you are asked to stay, ensure that your microphone is then muted for the rest of the hearing.

- If the family of the deceased have questions, the coroner may help the family with formatting and formulating these. This can be a complex and challenging situation for witnesses, but must be dealt with compassionately and with understanding.
A bereaved family, as part of the grieving process, may be looking for answers or even someone to blame. They may not have had access to all the information or been able to digest it, and so they may have filled in gaps with their own speculation or theories. At times, their loved one may have been let down by others and they are seeking to ensure no other family experiences what they have. The coroner or your legal representative will intervene if an inappropriate question is asked.
- The coroner and family are unlikely to be medically trained, so it is essential that you are clear and use ordinary language, as you have done in your statement. If the family go away understanding in simple terms what has happened, you have discharged your duties well.
- The style of questioning of barristers can feel intimidating and this can lead to a desire to end the interaction as quickly as possible, but try to avoid this feeling, as your input, in a considered and professional way, will be greatly valued, and the coroner will intervene if the style impedes your evidence.
- Unlike in criminal or disciplinary proceedings, where answering 'yes' or 'no' may deflect criticism, the opposite is likely to be true in an inquest. Repeated 'Yes' or 'No' answers may leave you vulnerable to being led by the person asking the question, and also risks being perceived as being defensive or less forthcoming, even if questions are being put to the witness encouraging such short answers. **The witness would wish to present themselves as an informed and reasonable professional, who knew what they were doing.** Although decisions are often made in a split-second, ideally the witness would be able to explain chronologically each stage in their decision-making process. It may be necessary to explain context if a question is unreasonable and challenge the premise of a question, which is not possible within a short 'yes' or 'no' answer.
- **'I don't know' or 'I don't remember' are acceptable answers.** It is crucial not to 'make it up' or guess or speculate. It is better to refer to what the relevant policy says or explain your usual practice.
- If appropriate, it is not unreasonable to give an opinion within your area of expertise or experience.
- Do not guess or make assumptions about what others did or might have done.
- If you are asked to comment or to deal with an area which is not within your expertise, then say so and decline to answer.
- As a professional witness, it is not appropriate to comment on the provision of a service or to criticise your colleagues. Remember, you may not have all the facts.
- **It is vital to think about your answer and to take time before responding.** You are there to explain what did and didn't happen, not to speculate about alternative scenarios, and the coroner will be mindful of this.
- Beware of pauses, do not be tempted to fill silences and do not give an opinion unless asked for it.
- Be yourself and do not be influenced by television programmes that you may have seen, as they often provide a dramatised representation.
- If there are no further questions, this is a good thing, as it means no further evidence is required.
- Once you have given your evidence and the coroner has thanked you, you can offer your condolences to the family if you have not done so already.

Advice on Managing Uncertainty

Inquests should be held within 6 months of the death (or at most 12 months). This can feel like a long time, especially for expectant families. You may have experienced an internal review or investigation and not wish to have to rehearse often painful events.

It is normal to have anxiety about appearing at an inquest, this is a natural human response to the thought of explaining the circumstances of a death even when there is no criticism of your actions.

If you have been criticised, by this point you will have already discussed your concerns with your legal representative and have been prepared fully, so you will be in the best position to explain clearly and compassionately what happened from your perspective.

Your previously submitted statement is not only a guide for the coroner, it is also a useful aide-memoire for you. However, your evidence is what you say orally on oath in the witness box, which may entail reading your statement out. This reinforces the point made in Chapter 9 that appropriate numbering of sections of your report is likely to make it easier to find the relevant sections quickly, and reduce the anxiety associated with fumbling through for the right part.

Remember you are not on trial at an inquest. It is already known that there has been a sad outcome; the inquest is there to understand the decision-making process. In some cases, the evidence may allay suspicions or concerns about bad practice, provide closure for the family and allow for fair reporting if the media is present.

If counsel (a barrister or group of barristers) has been instructed, the solicitor's role on the day will be to support any witnesses and the process, practically and emotionally. This ensures the inquest runs as smoothly as possible, while counsel does the advocacy.

For more guidance with regard to proceedings on the day, and on handling the stress of an inquiry, see Boxes 13.3 and 13.4.

Box 13.3 On the Day

- Be prepared, refresh your memory of events from your witness statement and from the clinical records, and bring all relevant documentation.
- Maintain a professional demeanour both outside and inside the court – nerves can make you laugh and smile inappropriately.
- The press may be at the court, as deaths in local hospitals and care organisations are often reported in local newspapers even where there are no criticisms, so be mindful that your conversations with others could be overheard.
- Arrive early, allowing extra time for travel and parking, and on arrival tell the coroner's officer who you are and which inquest you are attending.
- Remember your role is to assist the coroner and support families in finding closure by helping them understand what has happened. Acknowledge the family at the inquest – the inquest experience is very stressful and upsetting for them too.
- Try not to feel threatened or defensive, a calm and compassionate demeanour will help all navigate this often highly emotional process. It is ok to look upset.
- If family members or barristers ask questions in a confrontational manner, **do not become defensive**. Answer the question as fully and simply as possible.
- Listen to the question asked and answer the question asked clearly and concisely – not the question you would have liked to have been asked or the question that you believe follows on. If you have any comments on hearing other witnesses' evidence, pass these on to the legal representative.
- If you do not understand a question or it is outside your expertise, say so.

Box 13.4 Handling the Stress of an Inquiry

'I was called by the Medical Director as I was away from the ward and told to get straight back. The Medical Director was in a panic, which raised my anxiety. A tragedy had occurred. What followed was a year of paperwork and worry. An independent investigator was appointed, the report that was produced was very poor, it made a number of generic recommendations, which were not evidence-based. The inquest took place a year after the death, the staff were terrified, I was terrified. Someone had told me not to contact the family and I had naively followed that advice but was able to speak with them at the inquest.

The inquest was not difficult and did put a line under things but a few months later, I heard that the family had made a claim and received £5,000. That was the worst part, it really brought it home that someone had died, I couldn't stop thinking that a person's life was worth so little.'

Learning point: 'I initially spoke with my defence organisation and received some general advice via the phoneline and then asked to speak with an adviser, who had training in my specialty. That proved incredibly useful as they understood the systems and my fears fully. My advice would be to involve your defence organisation early.'

Giving Evidence

Nursing Perspectives

Stephanie Bridger, Sonya Clinch and Gillian Kelly

Key Points

- You are not expected to go through this process alone – seek support from your employer or trade union and the coroner's office.
- Stay calm and composed: focus on the facts and if there are things you don't have knowledge of or don't remember, just say so. If a question is unclear, don't hesitate to ask for clarification.
- It is crucial to know **all** parts of your role. Read the policy and/or procedures relating to your role(s) and ensure that you understand your responsibilities.
- You can best support the family to obtain some closure by remaining professional, preparing fully and showing empathy and compassion.

Many nurses will be asked to give evidence at a coroner's inquest during their nursing career. Being asked to give evidence can feel incredibly daunting and leave nurses feeling anxious and scared. It's important to remember that the coroner is looking for your help with the inquiry. The coroner can also seek an expert opinion by a nursing professional on the care of the person who has died.

Depending on the nurse's involvement in the case, a nurse may be called as either a witness of fact or as an 'interested person' (Chapter 7), and this will help inform whether or not the individual nurse is entitled to legal representation. Nurses called to give evidence should be supported by their employer and where nurses are members of a trade union, they can seek further advice and support from their respective union. Whatever the situation, nurses are not expected to go through this process alone. It is important for nurses to seek advice and take steps to ensure they get the support they need. In this chapter, we draw from personal experiences of inquests in coroner's courts and aim to set out key considerations for nurses who are called to give evidence.

Key Considerations for Nurses Who Have Been Called to Give Evidence

If your employer/Trust has assigned a solicitor to the case, make sure you get time to meet with the solicitor representing your employer/Trust. Whether your employer/Trust is or is not represented, which can be quite common, these are some key things to consider as part of your preparation.

Preparing Your Statement

Where a solicitor is assigned, they will usually help you write your statement and will go over it with you before it is submitted. If this is not available, a senior colleague, the Trust governance team or a defence organisation may assist. Where nurses are members of a trade union, they can seek further advice from their respective union. Some unions have a statement-checking team that can offer support (92). GP practices will have indemnity that covers all employees; this is usually provided by a defence organisation and most organisations have an advice line that can be contacted initially to discuss what support may be required, including reviewing and advising on your statement. Where a solicitor is assigned, they will also run through the process and questions that the coroner might ask of you. They are not allowed to coach you, but by making you aware of the questions you might be asked, it allows time for contemplation to prepare a considered answer. When writing your statement, keep to the facts and what your input was at that point in the patient's journey. Avoid medical jargon, do not speculate and avoid blame or personal opinions.

Court and tribunal hearings in England and Wales usually take place in public. This means you can observe them whether you're a journalist, an academic or a member of the public. You may find it helpful to attend a coroner's court to observe or shadow a colleague to better understand the legal proceedings and court etiquette, and have a general sense of what to expect.

Roles and Responsibilities

All qualified nurses need to be able to articulate their role and responsibilities; this is often an area that nurses are not always clear on. This may reflect the uniqueness of the nursing role, which includes proficiencies that apply to all registered nurses as well as roles and responsibilities specific to the nurse's specialist field(s). For example, the mental health nurse's role is different from that of a general nurse. However, for an inquest, understanding this and being able to clearly set out your role and responsibilities as a registered nurse in the context of your specialist field, as well as the professional standards nurses must uphold as part of the NMC Code (93), are key to being confident when giving evidence (94).

Nurses need to be really clear about the specific roles they hold and what is expected of them within these roles. It is crucial to know all parts of your role. For example: as an inpatient staff nurse you may also be the Primary Nurse for patients on your ward. Do you understand the Primary Nurse role and can you explain it? What does this mean in general terms and to you as a Primary Nurse? Have you read the policy and/or procedures relating to the role(s)? It is important to check if there is a Trust policy and/ or procedures relating to any role you hold because you will be asked about these policies, including your understanding of your responsibilities within it.

Incident Review and Clinical Records

If you have been called to give evidence at an inquest, request that you see the Patient Safety Incident Investigation Report (previously referred to as the Serious Incident Review Report). Find time to speak with the chair of the review report so you understand the learning and any recommendations that were made. After reading the report, look back in the clinical records about your input and what you did; sometimes it takes months for a case to get to an inquest stage – therefore, it is essential you go back to your clinical records to familiarise yourself with your input at that point and what your role was.

Your record-keeping is key, and you must know what have you written in the clinical records. Was it complete, factually correct and clear? The coroner will request the medical records prior to the inquest. You are just as important as any other witness, including more senior professionals, who will be on the stand giving evidence as well. Your clinical decision-making will be questioned, so remember to read through what you wrote at the time. This can help you in anticipating the questions you might be asked and allows you to prepare a factually accurate response. This is especially helpful in the event that your clinical records are not as clear or detailed as you would have liked and highlights why it is important to ensure good clinical record-keeping (93) at the point of entering them. You need to always document what you did, what you saw and your clinical opinion. Make sure before any inquest that you have read back through your clinical entries and that you are clear about what you are saying. The coroner or the family's solicitor will question you on what you have written. Be confident, but accurate. If you don't know the answer to the question, say you don't know. Do not try to make it up or, worse, lie. You are there to support the court in understanding what happened; if you can do this calmly and professionally, your input will be greatly appreciated by the coroner and the family. It is always a stressful situation, but remembering that you are not on trial can alleviate some of that stress.

Medical Emergencies

You may have been the first person to find the patient or you were the nurse in charge of the shift when the emergency took place. Either way, if you have been called to give evidence following a death on a ward and you were part of the response to the medical emergency, be sure to understand your role and skills at this point – for example, what training has been provided to you by the Trust and what exactly your role was during the emergency.

Deaths Following a Medication Error

On rare occasions, medication errors may result in the death of a patient and can lead to an inquest to determine the cause of death. Learning from inquests involving medication errors is crucial for improving safety. A careful evaluation of the circumstances will be required to ensure the safety of all patients. In the event of a medication error, it is important to take immediate and comprehensive actions. Policies within your practice or organisation set out guidance on the steps to take in the event of a medication error, which include: patient care; providing immediate medical attention to address the consequences and ensuring patient safety; reporting the error and notifying appropriate authorities; informing the family; open and honest communication about what has happened, as well as providing condolences and support; record-keeping; and thoroughly documenting the incident and actions taken, including preservation of the prescription chart, medical records and the medication itself, including any medical devices (i.e. infusion pumps) used to administer the medication, containers, labels and remaining medication in its original state. It is important to ensure that all records including the prescription are not altered and kept securely to enable full investigation of and learning from what has happened. Support for the staff involved is also crucially important as medication errors can result in considerable emotional distress to those involved. Following any medication error, the primary focus must be patient safety, transparency and taking steps to prevent recurrence of similar errors in the future.

Mental Health Considerations: Risk Assessments

Risk assessments are prevalent throughout all fields of nursing, but they are particularly important where a patient is suspected to have died by suicide and will bring scrutiny from the coroner or the solicitor acting on behalf of the family. Was the risk assessment up to date at the time? Were we clear about risks, were they clearly documented and was the risk assessment updated following *any* intervention with the patient? Whether this intervention was brief (a conversation in the corridor) or a more in-depth intervention (such as a formal consultation, period of engagement and observation or a thorough treatment in the emergency department), any known risks, including any protective factors, or any information that may reflect a change in risk, must be documented and any necessary action taken, including making any necessary changes to the risk formulation, risk management plan and/or care plan. Again, go back and check your clinical records for what happened at the time of the incident. If the family was involved in the care and treatment of the patient, did you document their comments and/or any concerns? Be able to talk about the importance of listening to and documenting carers' perspectives and concerns when they arise. This will be an area that could bring much attention. The Carers Trust Triangle of Care Standards (95) set out best practice in working together with the patient's family and friends.

Similarly, if you are working in the community, following a community suicide it is important to be able to recall details of your home visit or outpatient appointment with the patient. You may have been the last person to see the patient alive, so it is important to be able to talk clearly about your visit and/or appointment and your assessment of the patient's mental health at that point, including your risk assessment and the risk management plan. You may be asked about why a patient was not deemed as needing a hospital admission and it is important that you are able to justify your decision and refer to your risk assessment and management plans. We can never predict the future, but you can always document your decision-making at that point in time. Risk is fluid and can change quickly, so having accurate, comprehensive medical records is vital.

Absent without Leave from the Ward

Another area which is often scrutinised is that of a patient going missing from a psychiatric ward without permission to leave, known as going AWOL (absent without leave). Research has shown that patients who abscond from psychiatric inpatient units can be a significant risk to themselves and others (96). Similar risks can emerge for patients, who may be at risk to themselves, who unexpectedly leave or abscond from emergency departments or general hospital wards. It is important to be aware of your local Trust and/or regional AWOL policies and to ensure that the necessary actions are taken to safeguard the patient. Documenting all steps taken is essential. Carefully consider your role as the nurse in this scenario. Read the AWOL policy for your Trust/organisation. What is your role when a patient goes AWOL on your shift?

Understand your responsibilities if someone who is detained but who is given unescorted leave doesn't return. What did you do at that point? Re-read your clinical records and be able to articulate your decision to the coroner whatever that was; if it was a patient who often was late and you weren't concerned, be able to articulate that based on your knowledge of the patient and any associated clinical risks. If you weren't concerned about the patient, be able to describe why you weren't concerned. Again, check the AWOL policy for your Trust/organisation.

The Family

Inquests can feel daunting, but you are there in your professional capacity; you have touched the life of that patient while in your care and the family will be hoping for some closure. Be professional, and speak clearly and respectfully to the coroner, solicitor, patient's family or jury. You are not on trial, but your input is important to that family. If the family are representing themselves, which at times they do, you may be asked questions directly by a member of the family. There will be only one member of the family assigned to this role. It's important to remain calm and polite and to offer your condolences to the family. When families see that you genuinely care, and that you are compassionate and sensitive, it can provide much needed reassurance and be a vital part of the healing process; adding a crucial human touch to the legal proceedings can be helpful during what is a difficult time for everyone involved. The coroner will intervene if the questions are not appropriate or feel unprofessional and accusatory.

Confidentiality

While in the coroner's court, remember that there may be other services involved in the case, such as police, ambulance services, other Trusts and sometimes the media. Be mindful of your surroundings and the conversations you hold outside of the court room, but still within the building. Family, other members of the public and sometimes journalists will also be sharing the space with you, so remaining confidential and professional is paramount.

Understanding What Happened and Support

If the hearing is held over a few days (especially an Article 2 hearing – see Chapter 6), we recommend that you attend from the start. This will help you to understand the line of questioning from the barrister, solicitor, family or jury. It also helps you to see how other witnesses conduct themselves and answer questions. It gives you an idea of the line of questioning and the area of focus by the coroner. It is helpful to hold a session with the solicitor and other professionals involved from the Trust first thing in the morning before court starts and at the end of each day. This gives you valuable time to ask the solicitor acting on behalf of the Trust any questions you have or to address any concerns.

Once the inquest is over, you may feel emotionally drained. It is important to take time to recover. It is good to meet and reflect on the events and the outcome. This is best facilitated by a manager within your Trust/organisation so that support can be provided to staff and learning can be shared.

The key to feeling confident and prepared for an inquest is to be knowledgeable around the incident. Take time to understand the policies that weave through any actions you undertook as a registered nurse. Ensure you have read the Patient Safety Incident Investigation Report, have read your own clinical entries and reminded yourself of the events leading up to the incident, including your response to the incident and any statements you have provided to the court.

Taking part in an inquest is always a stressful situation; you may feel a great loss both personally and professionally, having invested in a relationship with a patient, and you will have to navigate the grief process, perhaps needing to seek support yourself. However, remembering the importance of the process for the family and that you are not on trial, and that the coroner is looking for your help with the inquiry, can alleviate some of that stress. Attending the coroner's court offers important opportunities to learn and develop and allows you to help the family understand what happened. You can do this best by remaining professional, preparing fully and showing empathy and compassion.

Chapter 5

The Roles of Advocates and the Jury in the Coroner's Court
A Legal Perspective

Emma Galland

Key Points

- There is no requirement for an interested person to be legally represented – this depends on analysis of the situation and the identified risks.
- Interested persons are entitled to disclosure of all documentation upon which the coroner intends to rely during the course of his/her investigation.
- The requirement of separate legal representation from your employer or organisation is very rare.

An inquest is an inquisitorial process, and this has an impact on the roles of the advocates and the jury, if there is one. This chapter explains their roles, and also when a professional may require separate legal representation, with some further tips on giving evidence from the perspective of a legal advocate with significant experience working in this area.

Advocates

An interested person (IP) *may* be represented by an advocate (either a solicitor or barrister) at the inquest. There is no requirement for an IP to be legally represented and representation will often depend on the identified risks. The considerations for whether legal representation may be warranted will include:

- the presence of other legal representatives;
- identified risks according to the circumstances of the case (e.g. if there are areas of care which could have been better);
- historic issues (i.e. if there are a number of deaths in similar circumstances);
- reputation: if there is already (or likely to be) media interest;
- potential civil claim; and
- requirement for witness support.

Role of an Advocate

The advocate's duty is to the court. It is not the role of an advocate in an inquest to 'put a client's case' to the court (this is different from other court proceedings). The inquest is an inquisitorial process – there are no 'sides' and no organisation/person has a 'case' to be put. Rather, it is therefore the role of the advocate to ensure that the coroner has all the information necessary to answer the four statutory questions and to conclude the inquest. In order to assist the coroner, the advocate will usually take the following steps:

Provision of Evidence

This usually takes place in advance of the hearing. This will include, for example, the provision of the medical records and/or relevant internal documents/policies. This will also include the provision of statements prepared by witnesses in order to assist the coroner in answering the four statutory questions.

In addition, the coroner has a duty under Regulation 28 of The Coroners (Investigation) Regulations 2013 (14) to write a report (also known as a Prevention of Future Death or PFD report) to any organisation that, in the coroner's view, may be able to take steps to prevent a death occurring in the future. It is important, therefore, that organisations provide evidence to the Trust of any learning. This may be by way of actions arising from an internal investigation and/or by way of setting out changes that have happened as a result of (or following, but not as a result of) the death. The advocate will usually assist in providing this evidence to the court.

Review of Evidence

IPs are entitled to disclosure of all documentation upon which the coroner intends to rely during the course of his/her investigation (14). Upon receipt of the disclosure from the coroner, the advocate will review the relevant documentation such that it affects his/her client. This is as part of the advocate's role to assist the coroner (e.g. to identify if there are any gaps in the evidence) and to assist the client and witnesses represented by that advocate to ensure that any issues are raised and can be addressed in advance of the hearing, if possible.

Hearing the Evidence

When the coroner and IPs (either separately or through their legal representatives) have reviewed the documentation, there will be consideration as to whether the evidence from a witness can be admitted as documentary evidence only (14), or whether the witness should be asked to give oral evidence. As a rule of thumb, the coroner will want to hear oral evidence from those directly involved in any incident which appears to have led to the death.

When hearing the evidence, the coroner will either ask the witness to read out his/her statement (either in whole or in part) or will ask questions of the witness effectively taking him/her through the statement. When the coroner has concluded his/her questions, the IPs (either individually or through their advocate) will be able to ask questions. These questions should be geared towards answering the statutory questions and should not be a rehearsal of the questions already asked by the coroner.

There is often some force in an advocate *not* asking questions – this is not because the advocate is lazy (or has fallen asleep!), but because the evidence is such that no clarification is necessary. As a general rule, evidence sounds far better coming from witnesses rather than being in response to an advocate's questions. However, there will be occasions when, entirely understandably, witnesses have got nervous and evidence has therefore become jumbled, or the evidence being given is highly technical and therefore some clarification may be necessary. This assistance can be provided by an IP's advocate through questions to the witness.

Assisting in respect of the Conclusion

While the findings of the coroner (or jury – see below) will be for the coroner (or jury) alone to reach, at the conclusion of the evidence the coroner will often ask for submissions from the advocates as to the conclusions available. Submissions should be on the law only and not on the facts. The submissions will be focused on advising the coroner of the conclusions available – or more frequently, not available – based on the evidence before the court. Speculation is not permitted.

The conclusions potentially available are either a short-form conclusion or a narrative conclusion, as noted in Chapter 6. While a short-form conclusion is often preferred, a narrative may be considered in situations which are either less straightforward (such that the conclusion does not sit within one of the short-form options available[1]) and/or involve a number of agencies. A narrative conclusion is a conclusion which would set out the central issues of the case which more than minimally, trivially or significantly contributed to the death.

The advocate may make a submission to the coroner as to whether a Regulation 28 report should be written and, if so, to which agency.

Separate Legal Representation

There can be very rare situations when either you will be advised to seek separate legal representation or you will wish to do so yourself. These situations could include when your views are not aligned with the organisation employing you at the time of the death or because there is a risk (either due to the facts of the case or because concerns have been expressed by others) of being referred to another agency (e.g. your professional regulator or the police).

While this is a difficult path to navigate, the purpose behind advising you to have separate legal representation is entirely for your benefit – so that you can have someone acting entirely on your behalf and with a view to consideration of any external agency involvement.

Even if separate legal representation is not required, if you are asked to provide a witness statement, it is entirely a matter for you as to whether you would like support in drafting that statement. Often, your defence organisation will be able to provide support in respect of the witness statement, even if not providing separate legal representation at the inquest.

The Jury: A Legal Perspective

The situations in which the coroner is required to empanel a jury is covered in Chapter 6.

The jury is often referred to as the unknown element of the inquest – jury members will often bring their own knowledge and experience to an inquest. While jury members would have been asked if there are any conflicts in the inquest (and will not remain on the

---

[1] Accident or misadventure; alcohol/drug related; industrial disease; lawful/unlawful killing; natural causes; open; road traffic collision; stillbirth; suicide.

jury if so), that will not stop people from having their own views. This may be because, for example, they have (or have had) a similar occupation to one involved in the incident or because a friend/family member has had some mental health concerns / has been in prison before. It is important, therefore, to keep evidence as clear, simple and succinct as possible. Juries return conclusions in an inquest based on the evidence before them.

Giving Evidence: Top Tips When Being Questioned by an Advocate

Below is a list of 'Dos' and 'Don'ts' when giving evidence to make the process as smooth as possible for you.

Dos

Dress smartly. These are court proceedings. As noted in Chapter 13, as a rule of thumb, you should wear business dress and muted colours.

Be prepared. Review your statement, the medical records and any relevant policies in advance of giving evidence and ask questions of your legal representative in advance. No question is too small – it is far better to address any questions/concerns in advance of the hearing.

Speak up and be clear. Often, the acoustics in court rooms are not ideal and it is important that the coroner, other IPs and the jury (if there is one) can hear you clearly. If you are naturally softly spoken, you are likely to need to concentrate on making sure that you can be heard.

Take your time. You will be nervous when giving evidence, especially if the family of the deceased is present. Before answering a question, ensure that you have understood the question (ask for it to be repeated if necessary) and know what you would want to say in response. Have a drink, take a breath and then answer the question.

Hold your ground. If something is suggested to you (e.g. action that you could/should have taken) and you do not agree with it, make that clear. Evidence in an inquest is what is said by witnesses / in documentary evidence. It is not the questions that are posed and you should feel confident in clarifying any specific points in your evidence.

Tell the truth. You will be giving evidence under oath. You will have promised to tell the truth, the whole truth and nothing but the truth. You must comply with this promise. Failure to do so may result in a referral to your regulatory body and/or criminal proceedings.

Don'ts

Waffle. Your evidence needs to be clear and understood. If you need to provide context to an answer, ensure that you answer the question first and then provide the context rather than the other way around.

Speculate. If you do not know the answer, then you should simply say that you do not know the answer. You should be giving your evidence based on the facts as known to you at the time of the incident/death rather than subsequent discussions. If a question is asked of you that should more appropriately be addressed with another witness (e.g. a colleague from a different specialism), then you should advise the court of this. If you do not recall the answer to a question, you should make that clear.

Guess. You should have access to the medical records and to your statement. If the information being asked of you is available in another document, you should ask to be able to refer to that document.

Be rude. This sounds obvious, but while the inquest is not adversarial, it can be uncomfortable when being questioned on your actions/omissions. Remain calm – you do not want to get into a fight with anyone, least of all the coroner or the family of the deceased.

Worry. Probably the most important tip. Yes, these are court proceedings and, yes, it can be a nerve-wracking process. However, there is plenty of support available. Any questions you have in advance of the hearing can be answered and any concerns you have can be alleviated.

Outcomes, including Regulation 28 Reports
Prevention of Future Death

Derek Winter and Gabrielle Pendlebury

Key Points

- Prevention of Future Death reports are not a punishment.
- If a problem or concern has been identified by an individual and/or an organisation in advance of an inquest, steps should be taken to address those issues, implement change, train and audit the steps taken.
- A Prevention of Future Death report raises concerns, but does not say how those concerns need to be addressed. They are not recommendations.

This chapter will briefly describe the outcomes of a coroner's inquest: the findings available to the coroner, and the types of concerns that they can express. It will also explain Regulation 28 (Prevention of Future Death) reports.

The Record of Inquest

... an inquest remains an inquisitorial and relatively summary process. It is not a surrogate public inquiry.
R (Morahan) *v*. Assistant Coroner for West London *[46]*

The coroner (or the jury, if there is one) will make a 'determination' of who the deceased was, how, when and where the deceased came by his or her death, and make 'findings' for registration purposes (4). The findings for registration purposes are the particulars required by the Births and Deaths Registration Act 1953 (14). The 'determination' and 'findings' must be recorded on the Record of Inquest (97) (Form 2 in the Coroners (Inquests) Rules 2013), which is then signed by the coroner and, if there is a jury, by those jurors who agree with it. This is a public document.

How a Conclusion Is Reached

The coroner (or the jury) is required to arrive at a conclusion by way of a three-stage process.
1. To make findings of fact based upon the evidence.
   When the coroner has heard all the evidence, they will give their decision with reasons (98) and deliver their conclusion (if there is a jury, they deliver the Record of Inquest).

2. To distil from the findings of fact 'how' the deceased came by his or her death and to record that briefly on the Record of Inquest.

   In most cases, 'how' means 'by what means' (11), usually a description of the mechanism of death. However, in Article 2 cases, 'how' means 'by what means and in what circumstances' (99). The coroner or jury must not include opinion other than on matters which are the subject of statutory determination (the Coroners and Justice Act (CJA) 2009 (4), section 5(3)) and they must not appear to determine any question of criminal liability on the part of a named person or civil liability (section 10(2)).

3. To record the conclusion, which must flow from and be consistent with 1 and 2 above, on the Record of Inquest.

Types of Conclusions

There are three types of conclusions: (1) a short-form conclusion; (2) a narrative conclusion; or (3) a combination of both. It is for the coroner to decide whether a short-form or a narrative conclusion (or a mixture) is more appropriate to the case in question.

The short-form conclusions noted in Chapter 6 appear in the notes to the Record of Inquest Form 2 that is scheduled to the Coroners (Inquests) Rules 2013 (14). A narrative conclusion is less restricted, going into more detail regarding the factual findings. For inquests where Article 2 has not been engaged, they are brief, neutral and non-judgemental.

In an Article 2 inquest, a short-form conclusion may be sufficient to enable the jury to express their conclusion on the central issues (100). However, frequently, a narrative conclusion will be required in order to satisfy the procedural requirement of Article 2, including, for example, a conclusion on the events leading up to the death, or on relevant procedures connected with the death.

The coroner may also return a conclusion which includes a rider of neglect in Article 2 and non-Article 2 inquests (using the words 'contributed to by neglect'). The relevant case is that of *R* v. *HM Coroner for North Humberside and Scunthorpe ex parte Jamieson* (11), where the court must be satisfied that the deceased was in a dependent position and that as a matter of law there is evidence of:

- a gross failure; and
- clear and direct causal connection between the gross failure and the death.

The definition of the term 'neglect' is set out in *Jamieson*, in which it was held that:

> Neglect in this context means a gross failure to provide adequate nourishment or liquid, or provide or procure basic medical attention or shelter or warmth for someone in a dependent position – because of youth, age, illness or incarceration – who cannot provide it for himself. Failure to provide medical attention for a dependent person whose physical condition is such as to show that he obviously needs it may amount to neglect. So, it may be if it is the dependent person's mental condition which obviously calls for medical attention (as it would, for example, if a mental nurse observed that a patient had a propensity to swallow razor blades and failed to report this propensity to a doctor, in a case where the patient had no intention to cause himself injury but did thereafter swallow razor blades with fatal results). In both the cases the crucial consideration will be what the dependent person's condition whether physical or mental appeared to be.

If an interested person (IP) has legal representation, the lawyer will be made aware of the outcome of the inquest and will communicate it to their client(s). If they are without legal representation, it is important that if the IP has left the court without knowing the outcome, then they should contact the coroner's office directly.

Health and social care professionals who give evidence may not learn the final outcome or not know that any criticism has been made about them or that a Prevention of Future Death report (see below) will be issued. If a professional works in an NHS Trust, then it is usual practice that their legal team or service would alert all witnesses to the outcome. However, for others, this might not occur, so ensure that you contact the coroner's office to obtain the outcome if you are not informed. Once an inquest concludes, the coroner cannot comment, and the only way to challenge its findings would be in the High Court, usually by way of a Judicial Review.

Regulation 28 Reports: Prevention of Future Death (PFDs)

Prevention of Future Death reports are not new (see Box 16.1). They help society to learn from deaths. Under paragraph 7, Schedule 5 of the CJA 2009 (4), and Regulations 28 and 29 of the Coroners (Investigations) Regulations 2013 (14), where an investigation gives rise to concern that future deaths will occur, and the investigating coroner is of the opinion that action should be taken to reduce the risk of death, the coroner *must* (a mandatory, not discretionary duty) make a report to the person the he/she believes may have the power to take such action. These Prevention of Future Death reports are known as PFDs (103).

PFDs are commonly feared or worried about by individuals and particularly organisations as 'things to be avoided', but it is important to realise that they are not a sanction. They are made for the benefit of the public and to provide comfort to families, by helping to prevent similar deaths occurring in the future. Many families tell coroners that they don't wish for another family to go through what they have endured. They do this by encouraging persons and organisations to make changes that would prevent such deaths. All PFDs must be copied to the Chief Coroner's office, as well as to persons or organisations who, in the coroner's opinion, should receive them.

The document should not contain personal information about the deceased, their family or others. Such details are unnecessary for understanding the learning points in

---

Box 16.1 Historical Perspective

The **Victoria Hall disaster** occurred on 16 June 1883 at the Victoria Hall in Sunderland, England. At the end of an entertainment show, gifts were distributed to children from the stage and it was announced that children with certain numbered tickets would be presented with a prize upon exit. This resulted in an estimated 1,100 children in the gallery rushing towards the staircase leading downstairs, in order to obtain gifts (101).

The door at the bottom of the staircase opened inward and had been bolted, leaving a gap only wide enough for one child to pass at a time. With nowhere to escape to, the children at the front were trapped and crushed to death by the weight of the crowd behind them, until the door was wrenched off its hinges (102). 183 children died.

An inquiry led to legislation that remains in place, that public entertainment venues be fitted with a minimum number of outward opening emergency exits, which led to the invention of 'push bar' emergency doors. No prosecutions resulted and the person responsible for bolting the door was never identified.

the report. An overview contained within a relatively short paragraph or two will usually be sufficient, followed by the specific points of concern.

PFDs are important, but they are not the main priority of an inquest (104) (in legal terms, they are ancillary to the coronial investigation). In an Article 2 inquest, the PFD may complete the state's duty to inquire fully (105), but a PFD is not mandatory simply because an inquest is an Article 2 inquest.

Whether a PFD report is required is often highly fact-sensitive and subjective, depending upon the circumstances of each individual case. A potential PFD recipient can implement an appropriate action plan to address the risk of future fatalities; this would mean that the coroner may not need to make a report if they have confidence that the action plan is being or will be implemented. This is a judicial decision for the coroner (not the jury if there is one) to make on a case-by-case basis, taking into consideration all the circumstances, but it is a matter for the coroner and they need not have any submissions of IPs regarding PDF matters (106).

The Coroner's Duty and Discretion in Issuing a PFD

The coroner's procedural obligation under Article 2 (to carry out an effective investigation into alleged breaches of its substantive limb) and the state's duty to inquire fully (105) can be supported or more easily demonstrated by a PFD, but it is not mandatory simply because an inquest is an Article 2 inquest (103).

The coroner's duty to issue a PFD arises in the following circumstances:

1. The coroner has been conducting an investigation into a person's death. Normally, the investigation will be complete, with the inquest concluded (but not necessarily, see below).
2. Something revealed by the investigation (including evidence at the inquest) gave rise to a concern. The matter giving rise to concern will usually be revealed by evidence at the inquest, but it may be something revealed at any stage of a coroner's investigation. The coroner is not restricted to matters revealed in evidence at the inquest.
3. The concern is that circumstances creating a risk of further deaths will occur, or will continue to exist, in the future (70).
4. In the coroner's opinion, action should be taken to prevent those circumstances happening again or to reduce the risk of death created by them.

If circumstances 1–4 apply, the coroner has a duty to report ('must report') the matter to a person or an organisation who the coroner believes may have power to take such action.

A family member or other organisation may believe that a PFD should have been issued when it was not. It is very difficult to challenge a coroner's refusal to issue a report to prevent future deaths. Although there is no coronial discretion, and a report is mandatory, if a coroner determines action should be taken to prevent a risk of future deaths continuing, the Divisional Court (*Dillon* v. *Assistant Coroner for Rutland & North Leicestershire* [107]) made clear that there is a significant subjective element in the decision-making process.

Different coroners could reasonably come to opposite valid opinions on the same facts. When a coroner considers issuing a PFD, there must firstly be a concern (arising from the investigation) that circumstances creating a risk of other deaths will occur or continue in the future. Then, the coroner must have formed the opinion that 'action should be taken' to prevent that risk of death. There is no single, objectively correct answer to the question as to whether 'action should be taken', thus making challenges very difficult.

In addition, no person has a right to be heard or to call any evidence that relates only to whether a report should be made. Coroners can choose to hear and give weight to representations by IPs, but this is at their discretion.

The Form of the PFD

The PFD is normally made after the inquest has concluded. This is because it is a pre-condition to making a PFD that 'the coroner has considered all the documents, evidence and information that in the opinion of the coroner is relevant to the investigation' (Regulation 28(3)). A PFD can be made before an inquest is heard if there is a need for urgent action, so long as the pre-condition is complied with (namely, the coroner takes the view that there is unlikely to be more material to come regarding the particular matter of concern).

A PFD raises concerns, but does not say how those concerns need to be addressed. The latter is a matter for the person or organisation to whom the PFD is directed. **PFDs are not recommendations.**

The coroner must send the report to 'a person who the coroner believes may have power to take such action', according to paragraph 7(1). 'Person' here can include an organisation as a whole. The report would usually be sent out within 10 working days of the end of the inquest. Once a PFD has been sent, the coroner has no power to withdraw it. See Box 16.2 for an example PFD.

On rare occasions, the duty to make a report does not arise as the matter does not relate to a risk of future deaths. In these circumstances, the coroner may write a letter expressing their concern to the relevant person or organisation. An example of this arose in the inquest into the death of Ian Tomlinson, who died during protests at the G20 summit in London in April 2009. There was evidence about police service vetting arrangements which did not relate to the death, but caused concern to the coroner. In due course, the Home Secretary amended the vetting arrangements.

Box 16.2 Example PFD

During the course of the inquest the evidence revealed matters giving rise to concern. In my opinion there is a risk that future deaths will occur unless action is taken. In the circumstances it is my statutory duty to report to you.

The MATTERS OF CONCERN are as follows:

1. the failure to arrange consultation between the mental health doctors and the doctors responsible for her physical health.
2. The failure to provide suitable or adequate care for her needs.
3. The failure to provide appropriate care.

In my opinion action should be taken to prevent future deaths and I believe that you have the power to take such action.

Sharing Reports and Responses

There is a very formal process for sharing both PFD reports and responses to them for wider learning. The coroner must send a copy of the report to the Chief Coroner and to all IPs who, in the coroner's opinion, should receive it (Regulation 28(4)(a)). Where the deceased is believed to be under 18, a copy must also be sent to the Local Safeguarding Children Board (Regulation 28(4)(b)).

A person or organisation must respond within 56 days, or longer if the coroner grants an extension (Regulation 29(4) and (5)). A response must detail the action taken or to be taken, whether in response to the report or otherwise, and the timetable for it, or it must explain why no action is proposed (Regulation 29(3)). A person or organisation giving a response to a PFD may make representations to the coroner about the release or publication of their response (Regulation 29(8)). Representations must be passed by the coroner to the Chief Coroner (Regulation 29(10)).

The Chief Coroner has a publication policy, including redactions (108), and may send a copy of a report or a response to any person they believe may find it useful or of interest (Regulations 28(5)(b) and 29(7)(b)). The coroner should consider requests for copies from other persons on a case-by-case basis. The Chief Coroner may publish a report or a response on the Courts and Tribunals Judiciary website (109).

If the inquest identifies a potential system failure that has regional or even national implications, a report to a relevant regional or national organisation may be needed. All reports and responses about deaths in prisons and other detention centres should as a matter of good practice be sent to HM Inspectorate of Prisons in all cases. They should also be sent to the HM Prison and Probation Service and to the Independent Advisory Panel on Deaths in Custody. Relevant PFDs and their responses should be sent to other organisations as well, such as the Department of Health and Social Care, the Health & Safety Investigation Branch, the Care Quality Commission, or the Department of Transport, so that wider lessons related to their services can also be learnt.

If a problem or concern has been identified by an individual and/or an organisation in advance of an inquest, steps should be taken to address those issues, implement change, train and audit the steps taken. See Box 16.3 for details of the Preventable Deaths Tracker.

Box 16.3 Preventable Deaths Tracker

Preventable Deaths Tracker is a database of PFDs to provide rapid analytics, identify trends and disseminate lessons. It is available at: https://preventabledeathstracker.net/database/coroner-names/

Managing Adverse Outcomes

Gabrielle Pendlebury and Derek Tracy

Key Points

- Early identification of risks allows for action plans to be developed and remediation to begin.
- Be proactive: chase information if required.
- Devise an action plan or a personal development plan to aid remediation.

Risk in inquests may be identified as an adverse outcome for an interested person (IP), a witness or a Trust or care provider. This could be a Prevention of Future Death Report (Chapter 16), a neglect finding, negative publicity or criticism as part of a narrative conclusion leading to involvement with your regulatory body or the Care Quality Commission (CQC). In rare cases, an inquest may be adjourned until the conclusion of any criminal proceedings (Chapter 8). Early identification of risks allows for action plans to be developed and remediation to be commenced, but on occasion, clinicians are still criticised by the coroner, and this can lead to a referral to their regulatory body, or a need to self-refer to their regulator. Self-referral to your regulator is not something you will do alone, but in conjunction with your indemnifier, governance department and potentially legal representative. This chapter will look at how to identify these risks. It will also consider what to do when criticism occurs, and how to remediate to allow for a satisfactory or moderated outcome.

The Coronial Request

Careful consideration of the initial request can help direct your statement. It is usual for the coroner to request 'statements from all clinicians involved in the care and treatment of the deceased', but if the coroner deviates from this, it can highlight areas that it is believed require more focus. This may be a specific time period or a series of attendances or consultations that could point to issues with sharing of information and discharge arrangements, or a specific specialty, such as tissue viability highlighting the need for consideration of any pathology related to that specialism.

If you are specifically named by the coroner in their request, for example, 'Please can Dr Smith provide a statement relating to the care he gave to X', it may be helpful to request directly or via your defence organisation or employer whether there are any specific concerns about the care that you provided and whether you or your organisation is an IP. This is useful information as you are then able to address those concerns in your statement. Appendix 2 shows a potential letter that your legal representative or defence organisation may send to the coroner to obtain information in anticipation of an inquest.

Cause of Death

The initial coronial request may not always provide a medical cause of death, but where it does, this should not be overlooked, as it may raise additional questions that would require discussion, review of any internal investigation for an NHS Trust, GP practice and so forth, and potentially steps to reduce risk of recurrence in that setting. For example, falls may be a result of environmental hazards on the ward.

Family Concerns

If the family have raised concerns, these will need to be addressed, and it is prudent to check with the coroner if this has occurred. In an NHS Trust, a legal team or service is likely to do this in most instances and alert any relevant clinicians. However, if a legal team is not available, the professional can contact the coroner's office directly; this can be done by calling or emailing the coroner's office yourself or by asking your defence organisation to do so. You are asking whether the family or others have raised any concerns about the care provided so that you have the opportunity to address these criticisms and thus support the coroner.

In some instances, there may be an ongoing local organisational or practice complaint or internal investigation. Understanding the issues identified in these may aid a comprehensive approach to the inquest, which through appropriate sharing of information will support the coroner in their investigation.

Incidents/Internal Review: Governance

In larger organisations such as NHS Trusts, local advisers, when considering a new coronial request, will link with the wider governance team and determine if the organisation has the need and capacity to review the outcome of any investigation/internal review or mortality review. The introduction of PSIRF (Chapter 4) and the changes inherent in that mean that such governance teams are taking a more proactive, data-driven role, and close liaison and collaboration will allow utilisation of their expertise to aid the process.

In any organisation or practice, pressures are numerous, so do not be afraid to chase information and make a call if emails go unanswered. It is important to identify a lead who will be responsible for this, especially in primary care.

Witness Statements

If you are an IP, you or your representative will analyse the witness evidence to consider if it covers the information requested and to identify any areas that may need clarification or evaluation. If you are merely a factual witness, you will not have access to all the witness evidence, so this analysis is not possible or required.

As noted earlier, identified concerns and problems with care should have been investigated internally, and any outcomes, particularly remediation, should be provided to the coroner and alerted to witnesses prior to the inquest.

There are a number of benefits to taking a systematic approach to identifying any risks early, both for the individual and the organisation. It prevents unnecessary surprises, so hopefully reducing the stress and impact of an inquest on those involved, allowing more time to prepare and instruct legal representation early, if required.

If an investigation is required, it can be started early, potentially allowing for new systems to be put in place and audited prior to the inquest. This would provide good evidence for any assurances or action plans that the coroner may consider to avoid a PFD or other adverse outcome. This is always easier when there is a governance team to support, which may not be the case for primary care or those in independent practice, but there is support and advice available from your indemnifier, your legal representative and potentially colleagues or practices who have implemented strategies and audit to improve systems.

Managing Adverse Outcomes

If issues with care are identified, a good approach would be to prepare the following:

1. An action plan detailing what needs to happen to prevent recurrence of issues in the future.
2. A statement assuring the coroner that anything that was said would be done has been completed, and if it hasn't been done, by when this should occur.
3. Selecting the most appropriate clinician to provide evidence to the coroner on this matter, should it be required. This may require some discussion among local clinicians, managers and the governance team.

Referral and Self-Referral to the Regulator

Self-referral to a regulator can lead to a multitude of conflicting emotions, but taking control of the process is psychologically beneficial and allows for remediation to begin immediately, thus putting the clinician in the optimum position for an early resolution.

In most professions, it would be anticipated that criticism by the coroner would be handled locally unless the coroner felt that involvement of the regulator was necessary. For example, the Nursing and Midwifery Council (NMC) does not require self-referral for criticism by a coroner and would wish that any matters could be dealt with locally by your employer, but this does not prohibit a coroner referring a nurse to the NMC (110).

However, in the case of medical professionals, paragraph 75 of *Good Medical Practice* highlights the requirement to inform the General Medical Council (GMC) without delay if you are criticised by an official inquiry; this would include criticism from a coroner in relation to an inquest (see Box 17.1). It is important to note that the GMC would typically consider a clinician making a self-referral as an indication of insight, rather than waiting for another, such as the coroner or Trust, to alert them to an issue.

Box 17.1 Good Medical Practice (111)

You must tell us without delay if, anywhere in the world:

a. you have accepted a caution from the police or been criticised by an official inquiry.
b. you have been charged with or found guilty of a criminal offence.
c. another professional body has made a finding against your registration as a result of fitness to practise procedures.

Remediation

The process of improving or correcting a situation.
Cambridge Dictionary

It must be highly relevant in determining if a doctor's fitness to practice is impaired that first his or her conduct which led to the charge **is easily remediable**, second that it has **been remedied** and third that it is highly **unlikely to be repeated.**
Cohen *v.* General Medical Council *(112), emphasis added*

Any professional who gets into difficulties should take active steps to overcome any perceived or actual shortcomings in their practice – namely, engage in the process of remediation.

Action Plan (Personal Development Plan)

A good step following criticism is to devise an action plan or personal development plan (Appendix 3). This is much easier with the assistance of suitably qualified and competent clinicians or other professionals, who are a step away from the emotion, so may be able to bring a practical approach.

A personal development plan is a useful step for the professional to take, in order to evidence their learning. It is not enough to merely attend a course and produce a certificate of attendance. Aims and objectives of courses attended should be set out in advance, with measurable outcomes that can be fully evidenced on completion. A diary of the steps and reflections taken over time can also be of assistance in evidencing learning; this is a very good way of also evidencing insight as the learning and reflections grow in complexity over time.

Box 17.2 A GMC Investigation Averted

A patient with a known history of ischaemic heart disease, previously under the care of a cardiologist and on maximal medical therapy, was seen with chest pain. An urgent referral was made to the same cardiologist, with a brief history in the referral letter and the intention of including previous correspondence/history as attachments. Unfortunately, the attachments were not included and the referral was triaged, without review of hospital records to 'routine'. The patient had a myocardial infarction and died before his appointment with the cardiologist.

At the inquest, legal representatives for the Trust and family proposed that had the intended attachments been sent, the referral would not have been downgraded and the patient would have been seen before his fatal heart attack. The coroner included this criticism in the final determination.

The doctor had a discussion with her defence organisation and was advised that the GMC must be notified as they were criticised by an official inquiry (114). She discussed the case with senior colleagues, who helped her to devise a personal development plan. She also reflected on the case and took steps within the practice to minimise the possibility of a similar oversight in the future. Her Responsible Officer was able to discuss the matter with the GMC employment liaison adviser (ELA). They were both reassured and the ELA indicated that a self-referral to the GMC was not necessary as remediation had been satisfactorily completed.

There was indeed no evidence of insight and remediation in this case. I do not much like those jargon words. They do not do much to illuminate the reality, which is that a doctor or other professional who has done wrong has to look at his or her conduct with a self-critical eye, acknowledge fault, say sorry and convince a panel that there is a real reason to believe he or she has learned a lesson from experience (113).

For an example of a case where a GMC investigation was averted after steps were taken to improve processes, see Box 17.2.

Chapter 18

Managing the Emotions around the Inquest Process and the Coroner's Court

Sian McIver, Sunita Shridhar and Shirley Tench*

Key Points

- The death of a patient and the subsequent inquest will have a different impact on each individual, depending on a multitude of factors.

Preparation is key and hopefully this book will have provided useful information to allow you to link with key people and develop a strategy. The emotional and practical impact on the professional and personal lives of those involved cannot be underestimated. This chapter considers the psychological and practical impact and provides some advice on managing often conflicting emotions. See Box 18.1 for some statistics surrounding inquests.

> ... the whole process took over 24 months in part due to the number of interested persons. It involved many hours of time for meetings to discuss actions, possible permutations, dissemination and audit of actions. During the course of this process, the stress involved was a factor in the resignation of one doctor from the partnership who no longer wanted to have the managerial responsibility and contributed to the resignation of a senior administrative member of staff.

If you have managerial responsibility, it is important to consider all those involved; some employees may be more vulnerable as they will not have had the training or experience of other professionals and may need further support.

There is a lot of provision available from various sources, including the coroner's office. Early liaison with the coroner and their office can often help reassure and prepare the professional for the inquest. The coroner can use his/her discretion and is well versed in handling sensitive information.

> The coroner asked me to go through my report into the medical and nursing treatment the patient had received and I did so in great detail. He asked for clarification on certain issues but did not ask why I thought the patient had killed himself. He thanked me for my evidence and praised me and the team for our care of the patient. He refused the family the option of cross examining me and ruled that the patient had killed himself whilst the balance of his mind had been disturbed. This was not necessarily the experience I had expected. I had heard of people being aggressively cross examined and undermined but the process I was a part of felt respectful and dignified whilst still trying to establish the truth.

---

* Note that the extracts in this chapter are from healthcare staff who have taken part in the inquest process, but who wish to remain anonymous.

Box 18.1 The Statistics

In 2022, there were 577,177 registered deaths in England and Wales, of which 208,430 were reported to the coroner, resulting in 36,273 inquests, with 476 of those (1 per cent) being held with a jury (115) and 403 resulting in a Prevention of Future Death report (1 per cent).

The Psychological Impact

It affected my work and family life; I was distracted, anxious, low in mood and a little agitated at times. I wondered what the family members would think of me, I was aware that grief can make people turn to anger and at times blame.

The death of a patient and the subsequent inquest will have a different impact on each individual, depending on a multitude of factors, but for some the psychological effect can lead to unexpected sequelae. It is important to recognise that you may need to do things a bit differently in the period after the death for your own health and wellbeing. Gibbons *et al.* (55) have suggested a number of strategies that may be helpful following the death of a patient by suicide. We have adapted these slightly to allow for applicability to all deaths.

The First Few Days

The death of your patient may come as a real shock to you. There are often many demands on professionals in the aftermath of a patient's death. You may need to carry out urgent duties alongside your normal ones and perhaps need a period of reflection for your own welfare. No matter how tempting it may be, while you are in shock, to want to set the medical records straight or speak to colleagues to make sure they agree with your version of events, do not do so. Not having perfect medical notes is common in a busy practice and generally understood by others, altering them retrospectively without making it clear it is a retrospective entry goes against professional standards and will not work out well.

Connect with the people in your natural support systems, such as family, friends, colleagues and communities. Talk to members of your family and close friends that you trust (within the limits of patient confidentiality), colleagues or a senior professional who can accompany you and offer you support. Talking with a colleague who has been through a similar experience or other clinicians involved in caring for the patient who has died can be beneficial. Early advice from your indemnifier can give you a road map of the next steps.

Look after your emotional health and physical health – you may need to be honest about the extent that this has impacted your emotional wellbeing and find a safe place to be able to express these feelings. In addition, make sure you don't neglect your self-care and try to maintain good sleep patterns, diet and exercise habits.

Seek help if needed. Some workplaces will offer formal or informal opportunities following a patient's death to talk through the events, but informal discussions with a colleague or friend can be valuable too.

Consider making temporary adjustments to your working patterns if you need time to process the death. A referral to Occupational Health might help put necessary measures in place if you need ongoing adjustment to your work pattern to support your recovery and to deliver safe patient care.

The Medium and Longer Term

If you are still having difficulties several weeks or months on or begin to have difficulties at a later stage, you may benefit from some additional support. There are many options for accessing support, but the first step is to recognise that you might need this and to let someone else know.

Signs that this may apply to you include the following:

- frequent intrusive thoughts about, or images of, the events around the death;
- nightmares and disturbed sleep;
- being more irritable, tearful or anxious;
- avoiding people or situations that remind you of the suicide, or where you may need to make difficult clinical decisions;
- taking longer than usual over work tasks, doubting your judgement or having difficulty concentrating;
- low mood;
- poor motivation;
- avoiding social contact;
- thinking about leaving psychiatry or medicine altogether; and
- maladaptive coping mechanisms, such as an increase in alcohol intake.

Concerns about confidentiality and not understanding the support structures available are key obstacles to seeking help. You may find it easier to speak to someone outside of your workplace initially. This may be a friend or relative, although your GP may also be a good starting point.

Consider seeking more formal professional help. This may be via NHS Practitioner Health, your GP, your organisation or private therapy.

The Inquest

The day of the inquest, I was very lucky to have the support of my manager; I cannot stress how helpful it was to have someone other than NHS solicitors support you through the process. I valued having another professional attend with me on the day of the coroners, sit with me before and after to debrief; I was given advice by him to remain 'level headed', not to become confrontational, and to remember that it was a fact-finding event and not to assign blame.

Chapter 13 gives advice on practical steps to undertake on the day of the inquest.

The thing that stays with me, always, is the pain of the family in court. I had made a prior diagnosis of a personality disorder on a young man who subsequently died by suicide. The family had been unaware of this diagnosis until his death, and challenged this, notably on the grounds that they disputed my assertion that he had self-harmed. My difficulty was that he had confided in me how he self-harmed in a way that compounded a deep inner sense of disgust and worthlessness. I was anxious that disclosure of this in court might enormously distress the family, and taint the memory of their loved one. I discussed this with the coroner in a pre-inquest hearing, and he was very sympathetic. When I was giving evidence, and was so challenged, the coroner intervened. He explained that he had spoken to me at length, and had been satisfied by my account of self-harm, but also that he believed that to discuss this in court might uncover information deeply distressing to the family, and which, in his opinion, had little direct impact on his death. I remember the family discussing this, and agreeing not to proceed with that line of questioning. I feel the right decision was made, and I counsel other professionals on potentially speaking to the coroner in advance if there is emotionally difficult material to cover. I still remember the deep hurt and sadness on the mother's face as she looked at me at that moment, and my sense of an inability to begin to imagine what she was going through and thinking.

Training

The purpose and framework of an inquest is not a subject that is regularly incorporated into the training of primary care staff. Many staff have never been involved in the process, do not know what to expect and how to conduct themselves at an inquest. This can lead to misunderstanding, and too often rumours about the experiences of others form a part of the narrative around expectations.

Trusts, legal service providers and medical indemnity organisations often run webinars and workshops on legal processes and have articles about how to write a statement for the coroner or prepare for an inquest.

It may be possible to shadow a colleague who is attending an inquest or speak with one who has attended an inquest. Even just visiting the court when an inquest is not taking place can be useful, as it can allow you to meet the coroner's officer.

Learn about local processes and ask for support.

I wrote directly to the coroner about the death of my partner and told him my concerns. Receiving a response and knowing that I had been taken seriously really helped me come to terms with my husband's death and what had happened.

Some tips for families from the Coroner's Support Service (116) are shown in the list below.

1. Try to appoint one family member or family friend to be a spokesperson for the family. Try to agree who this should be – divisions within the family can be distracting.
2. Write to the coroner in advance of the inquest setting out your main concerns. Try to be objective but firm. Doing this will help the coroner make sure he/she addresses all the important issues from the family's perspective and helps you work out in advance exactly what those issues are.
3. Ask the coroner, well in advance of the inquest to disclose relevant documents to you. The coroner does not always have to do this as some documents can be very upsetting. If you have a lawyer representing you, disclosure will usually be made to the lawyer.
4. Keep in touch with the coroner's officer, who will be your main contact (you will rarely get to see or speak to the coroner). The coroner's officer will usually give you all the practical information you need.
5. The inquest can be extremely upsetting and emotionally charged. But for some people, it can be very helpful as an important part of the grieving process. Think about taking a friend for support before, during and after the inquest.

Box 18.2   A Clinician's Perspective: What I Took Away

1. Be thorough in your clinical work. It is what is right for your patients and the team, but it will also stand you in good stead at an inquest. Get second opinions when you are in doubt and document discussions. You don't need to get everything right, but demonstrating you put attention to your care will help everyone at this point.
2. Write a really thorough report, not a long cut-and-paste job from the medical notes, but a comprehensive explanation for an intelligent lay person to explain what happened. Clarify jargon and medical issues so that the reader can understand what you did and why.
3. Use your defence organisation ahead of the hearing to make sure you have got the correct tone and information.
4. Work on your own feelings ahead of the inquest. While this may feel like an attack on your work, it is not really about you. It is about a family and wider society who have lost someone. If you stay stuck in your own resentment of the process it may well show under pressure. Your peer group or a trusted colleague who you don't feel you need to save face with can help with this.
5. It is unlikely to be as bad as you fear and, in most cases, provides closure for the family, allowing you and them to move forward with an understanding of events.

---

6. Children at inquests – usually children under 18 are not allowed to be at the inquest hearing or give evidence, this varies so check with the coroner's officer. In some cases, the coroner may permit this, but if you want children to attend you should ask the coroner's officer well in advance.
7. Press can be present at the inquest. You don't have to talk to them afterwards if you don't want to. But sometimes it may be just what you want. It is usually best to give yourself some time for reflection after the inquest before talking to the press.

Within the coroner's court I was challenged, by the deceased ex-partner, which was uncomfortable, however, I was supported by the coroner to ensure the questions were not accusatory. I was overwhelmed by her brother thanking me for my care and support, which I did not expect, I had focused on the negatives of attending the coroner's court.

For a clinician's perspective on inquests, see Box 18.2.

Although this book is for professionals, we can never be reminded too often that the family is always the centre of any inquest.

It was the end of a long day in the coroner's court. It had been emotionally trying, with several of our clinical team knowing the person who had died well, and having spoken at length on this and their care. There was almost an emotional catharsis as the coroner left the court and the day was done. Several of the team hugged each other, with mixed emotions of sadness and probably some relief. Movement caught my eye, and I saw a few feet away from us the husband of the deceased, who had been present all day and had asked questions of us and the care we had provided. He was gathering together the files he had, and walked past us silently but with what felt like a sense of dignity. I had a strong feeling of shame that I and my team had been so focused on ourselves and 'getting through' the day in court. We would leave, and our lives would continue; he left to go to an empty home, and a wife who would never return.

Appendix 1 Example Template for a Statement[1] for the Coroner

The Statement was prepared by [X] at the request of [X]

Re: Name of patient

Date of birth of patient

Date of death of patient

I am [full name]. My qualifications are [degree] from the University of [...] in [Year]. My further qualifications include [add any further qualifications]. I am currently working as [current position], a position I have held since [year].

I was involved in the care of [name of deceased] from [date] to [date].

This statement has been prepared on the basis of the contemporaneous medical records and from my memory of my involvement in [name of deceased]'s care.

[Patient's name]'s past medical history included [paragraph outlining past medical history of deceased, including all significant medical conditions and the dates they were diagnosed and any other relevant details, with a focus on past history which is relevant to the cause of death].

[Patient's name] was prescribed the following regular medications prior to their death [list of medications, including doses and indications, when started and stopped if relevant].

Paragraph summarising the background or history of the patient. There may be extensive medical records and taking time to represent this succinctly will produce a much more readable report compared to outlining every consultation.

An explanation of what happened in chronological order, explain medical terms and outline your involvement in the patient's care. The coroner will be most interested in those consultations/contacts close to the patient's death, so these should be more detailed than historical consultations that may be relevant to provide context.

Summarise the management of each of their conditions. If you wish to include details that are not recorded in the medical notes, be clear where this information has come from by beginning the paragraph with 'I recall that ...'. For the most relevant consultations, briefly outline the history, the examination findings, your working diagnosis and your rationale for that diagnosis. Outline your management plan and any follow-up that was arranged. If you are describing a consultation that the patient had with another clinician, include their full name. Include any risk assessments and risk formulations in psychiatric cases to help understand the rationale behind decisions.

List and explain, if necessary, all relevant referrals and whether the patient was under the care of specialist or other services at the time of or close to their death.

The final consultation will generally be the most important: I last saw [name of deceased] on [date], when [he/she] presented with [include here a more detailed description of your last consultation/ interaction with the patient, including history and examination, diagnosis and management plan].

Answer any specific questions which have been asked by the coroner – a separate paragraph for each question.

My last involvement with [name of deceased] was on [date]. I heard of his/ her death on [date]. [You may also want

---

[1] Sometimes called a report.

to make comment if anything significant occurred subsequent to your last consultation].

I believe that the facts and matters contained in this statement are true.

I would like to offer my sincere condolences to the family and friends of [name of deceased], for their loss.

I hope the information in this report has been of assistance to the coroner. I would be happy to provide further information or clarification, should it be required.

Signed:
[Writer's name and date]

Appendix 2 Example Letter that Your Legal Representative or Defence Organisation May Send to the Coroner Requesting Information

Dear **Coroner,**

I understand that I have been called to give evidence in the inquest touching on the death of [name of deceased]. I respectfully request the following further information concerning the inquest so that I am fully prepared:

1. the time at which the inquest is scheduled to begin;
2. the length of time for which the inquest has been scheduled;
3. the status in which I have been called, whether I am a Factual Witness or Interested Person;
4. if I am an Interested Person, I would be grateful if you could advise under which sub-section of section 47(2) of the Coroners and Justice Act 2009 this decision has been made;
5. any criticisms which have been made of the care provided to the deceased by myself which you are aware of;
6. whether any expert evidence is being called (please provide the name and area of expertise);
7. whether any witnesses are being called (please provide their names and relation to the case);
8. whether any parties will be legally represented at the hearing (please provide the names of the legal representatives and the name of their law firm/chambers);
9. whether I am entitled to any advanced disclosure.

I look forward to receiving this information.

Yours sincerely,
[Writer's name]

Appendix 3 Personal Development Plan

The plan will evolve; it should be updated whenever there has been a change – either when a goal is achieved or modified, or where a new need is identified.

My development needs	Actions to address them	Date that I plan to achieve the development goal	Proposed outcome	Completion
List the learning need and explain how it was identified.	Outline the type of learning you will undertake.	Set an appropriate timescale for achieving the development goal.	How will this impact on and change your practice as a result of the development activity?	Evidence for completion and reflection on your learning. Also outline any new learning needs identified as a result of previous learning.
1				
2				
3				
4				
5				

References

1 The National Archives (ed.). Notification of Deaths Regulations 2019.

2 Ministry of Justice. Guidance for Registered Medical Practitioners on the Notification of Deaths Regulations (2022).

3 HM Passport Office. Guidance for Doctors Completing Medical Certificates of Cause of Death in England and Wales (accessible version) (2022).

4 The National Archives (ed.). Coroners and Justice Act 2009.

5 Courts and Tribunals Judiciary. Legislation and Statutory Instruments (2024).

6 Holdsworth, W. S. *A History of English Law* (Sweet & Maxwell Ltd, 1956), Vol. 1, pp. 82–3.

7 Select Coroners' Rolls (Selden Society), Vol. 9, p. xxiv.

8 Duggan, K. F. The Hue and Cry in Thirteenth-Century England, in A. Spencer and C. Watkins (eds), *Thirteenth Century England XVI* (Boydell Press, 2017), pp. 153–72.

9 The Coroners' Society of England and Wales. History (2024). Available at: www
.coronersociety.org.uk/the-coroners-society/history/#:~:text=The%20fine%
20was%20known%20as,the%20%
27Presentment%20of%20Englishry%27

10 His Honour Judge Peter Thornton KC Chief Coroner (ed.). The Coroner System in the 21st Century: The Howard League for Penal Reform – Parmoor Lecture (25 October 2012).

11 R v. HM Coroner for North Humberside and Scunthorpe ex parte Jamieson [1995] 1 QB 1, 26.

12 Judicial Review and Courts Bill (UK Parliament, London, 2022).

13 Courts and Tribunals Judiciary. Chief Coroner's Guidance No. 6: The Appointment of Coroners (2020).

14 The National Archives. The Coroners (Inquests) Rules 2013 (2013). Available at: www.legislation.gov.uk/uksi/2013/1616/made

15 Public Health England. Guidance: Duty of Candour (London, 2020). Available at: www.gov.uk/government/publications/nhs-screening-programmes-duty-of-candour/duty-of-candour

16 NHS England. National Guidance on Learning from Deaths (2017).

17 NHS England. Patient Safety Incident Response Framework (2023).

18 Health Services Safety Investigations Body website. Available at: www.hssib.org.uk/

19 NHS England. Patient Safety Incident Investigation (2022).

20 NHS England. Swarm Huddle (2022).

21 NHS England. Guide to Responding Proportionately to Patient Safety Incidents (2022).

22 NHS Improvement. Never Events List 2018 (London, 2021).

23 NHS England. Engaging and Involving Patients, Families and Staff Following a Patient Safety Incident (London, 2022).

24 NHS England. Patient Safety Incident Response Framework Supporting Guidance: Oversight Roles and Responsibilities Specification (London, 2022).

25 NHS England. Patient Safety Incident Response Standards (London, 2022).

26 R (AP) v. HM Coroner Worcestershire [2001] EWHC 1453 QB (Admin).

27 NHS England. Patient Safety Incident Response Framework: Preparation Guide (London, 2022).

28 NHS England. SEIPS Quick Reference Guide and Work System Explorer (London, 2022).

29 NHS England. NHS Patient Safety Syllabus Training Programme (London, 2024).

30 NHS England. A Just Culture Guide (London, 2023).

31 Ministry of Justice. Guidance for Registered Medical Practitioners on the Notification of Deaths Regulations (London, 2022).

32 R (Linnane) v. HM Coroner for Inner North London [1989] 1 WLR 395.

33 The Medical Examiners (England) Regulations 2024. Available at: www .legislation.gov.uk/uksi/2024/493/ contents/made

34 Gunn, J. Dr Harold Frederick Shipman: An Enigma. *Crim. Behav. Ment. Health* **20**, 190–198 (2010).

35 Bloom v. ADC North London v. Whipps Cross Hospital [2004] EWHC 3071 (Admin).

36 R v. Poplar Coroner ex parte Thomas, 15 December 1992, CA.

37 R (Touche) v. Inner North London Coroner [2001] EWCA Civ 38.

38 R v. HM coroner for Birmingham and Solihull ex parte Benton (1997) 162 JP 807.

39 Savage v. South Essex Partnership NHS Trust [2008] UKHL 74.

40 Mills & Reeve. Briefing. Coroner's Inquests: Outcomes (2019).

41 Supreme Court in [2012] UKSC 2. On appeal from [2010] EWCA Civ 698 (2012).

42 Bray, R. S. Paradoxical Justice: The Case of Ian Tomlinson. *J. Law Med.* **21**, 447–72 (2013).

43 England and Wales High Court (Administrative Court) Decisions (2021).

44 R (Letts) v. Lord Chancellor [2015] EWHC 402 (Admin).

45 Rabone v. Pennine Care NHS Trust [2012] UKSC 2.

46 R (Morahan) v. Assistant Coroner for West London [2022] EWCA Civ 1410.

47 R (on the application of Maguire) (Appellant) v. His Majesty's Senior Coroner for Blackpool & Fylde and another (Respondents) [2023] UKSC 20.

48 Supreme Court. Press summary: R (on the application of Maguire) (Appellant) v His Majesty's Senior Coroner for Blackpool & Fylde and another (Respondents) [2023] UKSC 20 (2021). Available at: www.supremecourt.uk/ press-summary/uksc-2021-0038.html

49 Ministry of Justice. National Statistics: Coroners Statistics 2022: England and Wales (London, 2023).

50 R v. Coroner for Southern District of Greater London ex parte Driscoll (1993) JP 45 DC at [40], referring to r. 20(2)(h) of the Coroners Rules 1984, the predecessor to s. 47(2)(m).

51 Courts and Tribunals Judiciary. Judicial Review (2023).

52 Sandford, D. M., Kirtley, O. J., Thwaites, R. and O'Connor, R. C. The Impact on Mental Health Practitioners of the Death of a Patient by Suicide: A Systematic Review. *Clin. Psychol. Psychother.* **28**, 261–94 (2021).

53 Campbell, D. and Hale, R. *Working in the Dark: Understanding the Pre-Suicide State of Mind* (Routledge, 2017).

54 National Institute for Health and Care Excellence. Self-Harm: Assessment, Management and Preventing Recurrence (London, 2022).

55 University of Oxford Centre for Suicide Research. If a Patient Dies by Suicide: A Resource for Psychiatrists (Oxford, 2020).

56 R (on the application of Thomas Maughan) v. HM Senior Coroner for Oxfordshire (2020) UKSC 46.

57 Chief Coroner. Law Sheet 6. R (on the application of Maughan) v. HM Senior Coroner for Oxfordshire [2020] UKSC 46 (2020).

58 R (Wilkinson) v. HM Coroner for Greater Manchester South District [2012] EWHC 2755 (Admin) at [70].

59 R v. Rose [2017] EWCA Crim 1168.

60 Office for National Statistics. Crime in England and Wales: Year Ending March 2023 (London, 2023).

61 Ng, L., Merry, A. F., Paterson, R. and Merry, S. N. Families of Victims of

Homicide: Qualitative Study of Their Experiences with Mental Health Inquiries. *BJPsych. Open* **6**, e100 (2020).

63 ITN. Timeline: The Jack Adcock Case So Far (London, 2015). Available at: www.itv.com/news/central/2015-11-04/timeline-jack-adcock-trial

64 The Coroners (Inquest) Rules 2013, Rule 25(4).

65 General Medical Council. Good Medical Practice (London, 2024).

66 General Medical Council. Confidentiality: Good Practice in Handling Patient Information (London, 2017).

67 Chief Coroner. Guidance No. 22: Pre-Inquest Review Hearings (2020). Available at: www.judiciary.uk/wp-content/uploads/2020/08/guidance-no-22-pre-inquest-review-hearings.pdf

68 Coroner for the Birmingham Inquests (1974) v. Hambleton and Others [2018] EWCA Civ 2081.

69 Speck v. HM Coroner for District of York and Others [2016] EWHC 6.

70 Coroners Inquests into the London Bombings of 7 July 2005, per Lady Justice Heather Hallett, Assistant Deputy Coroner for Inner West London, ruling 6 May 2011, transcript p. 15.

71 Fullick v. HM Coroner for Inner North London and Others [2015] EWHC 3522.

72 Fullick v. HM Coroner for Inner North London and Others [2015] EWHC 3522 (Admin); Paul v. Deputy Coroner for the Queen's Household and the Assistant Deputy Coroner for Surrey [2007] EWHC 408 (Admin).

73 R (Hair) v. HM Coroner for South Staffordshire [2010] EWHC 2580 (Admin).

74 R (Mack) v. HM Coroner for Birmingham and Solihull [2011] EWCA (Civ) 712.

75 BMA. Coroners' Court Fees and Allowances (2023). Available at: www.bma.org.uk/pay-and-contracts/fees/fees-for-doctors-services/coroners-court-fees-and-allowances

76 R v. Lawrence [2019] Wimbledon Magistrates Court.

77 Rix, K., Mynors-Wallis, L. and Craven, C. *Rix's Expert Psychiatric Evidence* (Cambridge University Press, 2021).

78 McKerr v. Armagh Coroner [1990] 1 WLR 649.

79 R v. Southwark Coroner, ex parte Fields (1998) 162 JP 411.

80 R (Ahmed) v. South and East Cumbria Coroner [2009] EWHC 1653 (Admin); Mack v. HM Coroner for Birmingham [2011] EWCA Civ 712 (CA).

81 R (Takoushis) v. Inner North London Coroner [2006] 1 WLR 461; R (LePage) v. HM Assistant Deputy Coroner for Inner South London [2012] EWHC 1485 (Admin).

82 Chambers v. HM Coroner for Preston and West Lancashire [2015] EWHC 31 (Admin).

83 R (Takoushis) v. HM Coroner for Inner North London [2005] EWCA Civ 1440.

84 R v. HM Coroner for East Sussex Western District, ex parte Homberg [1994] 1 WLUK 555.

85 R v. HM Coroner for Inner London West District, ex parte Dallaglio [1994] 4 All ER 139.

86 Re Bithell (Deceased) [1986] 1 WLUK 114.

87 The National Archives. The Coroners Allowances, Fees and Expenses Regulations 2013 (2013).

88 Courts and Tribunals Judiciary. Chief Coroner's Guidance No. 25: Coroners and the Media (2016).

89 Ministry of Justice. Proposals to Allow the Broadcasting, Filming, and Recording of Selected Court Proceedings (London, 2012).

90 Chief Coroner. Chief Coroner's Guidance No. 41 Use of 'Pen Portrait' Material (London: Courts and Tribunals Judiciary, 2021). Available at: www.judiciary.uk/wp-content/uploads/2021/07/Chief-Coroners-Guidance-No-41-Use-of-Pen-Portrait-material.pdf

91   Chief Coroner. Chief Coroner's Guidance No. 42: Remote Hearings. (London: Courts and Tribunals Judiciary, 2022).

92   Royal College of Nursing. Statements: How to Write Them (2023). Available at: www.rcn.org.uk/Get-Help/RCN-advice/statements

93   Nursing and Midwifery Council. Future Nurse: Standards of Proficiency for Registered Nurses (London, 2018).

94   NHS Resolution. Giving Evidence at Inquest: A Well Prepared Witness (London, 2020).

95   Carers Trust. Resources (2024). Available at: https://carers.org/resources/all-resources

96   NCISH. Annual Report 2023: UK Patient and General Population Data 2010–2020 (Manchester: University of Manchester, 2023).

97   Chief Coroner. Chief Coroner's Guidance No. 17: Conclusions: Short-Form and Narrative (London: Courts and Tribunals Judiciary, 2021).

98   R (Lewis) v. Senior Coroner NW Kent [2020] EWHC 471 (Admin).

99   R (Middleton) v. HM Coroner for West Somerset [2004] 2 AC 182.

100 McCann v. United Kingdom (1995) 21 EHRR 97.

101 'Victims of the Victoria Hall Calamity'. Genuki. Archived from the original on 17 November 2015.

102 Stoner, S. Children's Deaths that Shocked the World. Sunderland Echo (2008).

103 Chief Coroner. Revised Chief Coroner's Guidance No. 5: Reports to Prevent Future Deaths (London: Courts and Tribunals Judiciary, 2020). Available at: www.judiciary.uk/guidance-and-resources/revised-chief-coroners-guidance-no-5-reports-to-prevent-future-deathsi/

104 Re Kelly (deceased) (1996) 161 JP 417.

105 R (Lewis) v. HM Coroner for the Mid and North Division of the County of Shropshire [2009] EWCA Civ 1403.

106 R (Gorani) v. Her Majesty's Assistant Coroner for Inner West London and Others [2022] EWHC 1593 (QB).

107 Dillon v. Assistant Coroner for Rutland & North Leicestershire [2022] EWHC 3186 KB (Admin).

108 Chief Coroner. Prevention of Future Deaths Reports: Publication Policy (2021).

109 Courts and Tribunals Judiciary. Prevention of Future Death Reports (2024). Available at: www.judiciary.uk/?s=&pfd_report_type=&post_type=pfd&order=relevance

110 Nursing and Midwifery Council. Making a Self-Referral (2022). Available at: www.nmc.org.uk/concerns-nurses-midwives/information-for-registrants/self-referrals

111 General Medical Council. Domain 4: Maintaining Trust (2024). Available at: www.gmc-uk.org/professional-standards/professional-standards-for-doctors/good-medical-practice/domain-4-trust-and-professionalism

112 Cohen v. General Medical Council [2008] EWHC 581 (Admin) at [65].

113 Kimmance v. General Medical Council [2016] EWHC 1808 (Admin), Kerr J.

114 General Medical Council. Reporting Criminal and Regulatory Proceedings within and outside the UK (2024). Available at: www.gmc-uk.org/ethical-guidance/ethical-guidance-for-doctors/reporting-criminal-and-regulatory-proceedings-within-and-outside-the-uk/reporting-criminal-and-regulatory-proceedings-within-and-outside-the-uk

115 Ministry of Justice. Coroners Statistics 2022: England and Wales – Inquests Opened (London, 2023).

116 The Coroners' Courts Support Service website. Available at: https://coronerscourtssupportservice.org.uk/

Index

Printed in the United States
by Baker & Taylor Publisher Services